BODYBUILDING
FOR BEGINNERS

BODYBUILDING
FOR BEGINNERS

BILL REYNOLDS

CONTEMPORARY
BOOKS, INC.
CHICAGO • NEW YORK

Library of Congress Cataloging in Publication Data

Reynolds, Bill.
Bodybuilding for beginners.

Includes index.
1. Bodybuilding. I. Title. II. Title: Body-building for beginners.
GV546.5.R48 1983 646.7'5 83-10051
ISBN 0-8092-5499-9

Exercise photos by Bill Reynolds.

Published by Contemporary Books, Inc.
180 North Michigan Avenue, Chicago, Illinois 60601
Manufactured in the United States of America
Library of Congress Catalog Card Number: 83-10051
International Standard Book Number: 0-8092-5499-9

Published simultaneously in Canada by Beaverbooks, Ltd.
195 Allstate Parkway, Valleywood Business Park
Markham, Ontario L3R 4T8 Canada

Contents

Foreword

You have in your hands the best basic bodybuilding training manual that I have ever seen. Bill Reynolds has spared no efforts in making *Bodybuilding for Beginners* an informative and inspiring book for both men and women of all ages. I firmly believe that I would have saved at least a year of unproductive training if I had had this book when I began bodybuilding back home in Sweden.

It's essential that you learn the correct way to train at the beginning of your involvement with bodybuilding, because it's very difficult to change bad habits later in your career. And, after reading the manuscript for *Bodybuilding for Beginners* and reviewing the exercise photos that go with it, I am convinced you will be able to learn proper exercise habits with no more coaching than is provided by this book.

I've known Bill Reynolds for many years and have come to view his knowledge of bodybuilding with great respect. His mind is like a computer bank when it comes to bodybuilding, and he has always given me good advice.

Bill has trained with many champion bodybuilders—men and women alike—and has interviewed many more, so you can be assured that he knows how all of the elite bodybuilders train. He is also thoroughly familiar with how individual bodies respond uniquely to different philosophies of bodybuilding training. Few if any bodybuilding experts can match Bill's knowledge of the sport, so you can't ask for a better instructor.

Bodybuilding for Beginners has my highest recommendation. Follow the instructions in this book to the letter, and you will dramatically improve your physique in a relatively short time. Good luck with your workouts!

Andreas Cahling,
IFBB Mr. International

BODYBUILDING
FOR BEGINNERS

1

Bodybuilder!

Bodybuilding! Through the film and television appearances of Lou Ferrigno, Arnold Schwarzenegger, and many others, the sport has gained greater and greater public acceptance during the late 1970s and early 1980s. Hundreds of thousands of men and women who wouldn't have been training with weights to reshape their bodies just a few years ago are now pumping iron in gyms all over America, Canada, and the rest of the world.

Bodybuilding has grown so rapidly in recent years that it is now the world's seventh most popular sport. This ranking is based on the fact that 117 countries currently have national bodybuilding federations affiliated with the International Federation of Bodybuilders. Indeed, bodybuilding has grown so quickly that it is now possible that the sport will soon be included in the Olympic Games.

Bodybuilder! The sport of bodybuilding is so demanding that any man or woman who wins a title is an exceptional athlete. A champion bodybuilder can withstand the rigors of training two or three hours per day, often when his or her energy reserves are depleted by precontest dieting. Few athletes are as disciplined as a bodybuilder must be in diet and training.

Bodybuilding workouts are painful, because all bodybuilders learn to push themselves past a pain barrier erected by body fatigue. The guiding axiom in competitive bodybuilding is "No pain, no gain." As a result, elite bodybuilders frequently joke about being participants in "the sport of masochists."

Since it is such a rigorous athletic endeavor, bodybuilding attracts a rare breed of men and women. It also gives people qualities that make them even more successful in life. Bodybuilding gradually develops a high degree of personal character, will power and self-discipline, qualities that carry over quite profitably into other aspects of life.

Generally speaking, the best bodybuilders have developed personal attributes that make them better students, better businesspeople, better athletes in other sports, and better individuals in every other facet of life. The IFBB motto—"Bodybuilding is good for nation building"—also means that bodybuilding is good for person building.

Henry Wadsworth Longfellow, the great American poet, unwittingly capsulized the pleasure of being a bodybuilder more than a century ago when he wrote the following stanza in his "The Light of Stars":

> Oh, fear not in a world like this,
> And thou shalt know erelong,
> Know how sublime a thing it is
> To suffer and be strong.

Do you have what it takes to become a successful bodybuilder? Do you want more than anything else in life to become a champion? I'm sure that you do, and in this book I intend to help you set your feet on the path to proper training and diet so you can soon maximize your bodybuilding potential.

WHY THIS BOOK?

I've been personally involved in weight training and bodybuilding since 1960. For eight years I was a moderately successful competitive bodybuilder, and for five years, I taught weight training to college-age students. Since 1967 I've been writing articles on bodybuilding, and since early 1978 I have been the editor-in-chief of *Muscle & Fitness* magazine, the world's leading bodybuilding journal.

Over the years I've interviewed and/or trained with virtually every champion male and female bodybuilder. And, along the way, it's been my pleasure to instruct hundreds of beginning bodybuilders.

My experience in the sport has convinced me that bodybuilding novices are confronted by such a bewildering array of information that they soon feel like they're wandering lost in an Amazon jungle. There are scores of weight training and bodybuilding books on the market, more than 20 of which I've personally written or edited. At least 10 bodybuilding magazines are available at newsstands, and hundreds of bodybuilding authorities stand waiting to fill a novice bodybuilder's ears.

There's little wonder that a beginning bodybuilder ends up confused about how to train and eat! I wrote this book specifically to give you a road map through the confusing jungles of information and misinformation that will confront you. Using this book, you can follow a freeway to success rather than a faint and winding jungle path with hundreds of dead ends.

If you read this book carefully, you'll learn correct exercise procedures and dietary habits from the start, which will save you months—perhaps even years!—of fruitless effort.

I spent nearly a year compiling information and writing *Bodybuilding for Beginners* to give you the best chance of succeeding as a bodybuilder.

Bodybuilding for Beginners will give you a solid framework of knowledge, which you can gradually flesh out with more sophisticated techniques by reading the books and magazines recommended in Chapter 7.

This book should be used as a road map to bodybuilding success. With *Bodybuilding for Beginners* as your first coach, you *can* become a champion bodybuilder in a short time and with a minimum of confusion.

TWO PATHS TO FOLLOW

Bodybuilding is one of several subdivisions of the general physical activity called *weight training*. Occasionally referred to as *progressive resistance exercise*, weight training is a form of muscular exercise that uses the resistance provided by free weights (e.g., barbells, dumbbells, and related equipment) and a variety of exercise machines.

Most commonly, bodybuilding involves using weight training and healthy nutritional practices to reshape the body. Literally millions of men and women use this mild form of bodybuilding to build up an under-par muscle group or two or to generally slim and tone their bodies. Competitive bodybuilders often refer to this activity as *bodyshaping* to differentiate it from their more serious endeavor.

If your goal is bodyshaping, almost all of the information presented in this book will be of value to you. In shaping your body, you can use the training tips discussed in Chapters 2 and 5, the exercises explained in Chapter 3, and the first four training routines presented in Chapter 4. These four routines will allow you to reshape your body rapidly, after which you can follow the body maintenance program included in Chapter 4 to retain the well-shaped, physically fit physique you've developed.

While bodyshaping is certainly a worthwhile endeavor, most of you will be interested in preparing for bodybuilding competition. If you plan to become a bodybuilding competitor, you should digest and assimilate every word in this book. *Bodybuilding for Beginners* will give you the information, exercises, and routines needed for use during your initial four to six months of bodybuilding training.

As a future competitive bodybuilder, you will complete the beginning phase of training and push well into the intermediate phase with the knowledge you gain in using this book. You will make very noticeable improvements in your physique during the months that you train using the instructions presented in *Bodybuilding for Beginners*. And the momentum you generate in your first few months of training will help you push more quickly to the top.

Prospective competitive bodybuilders, then, should use this book to build a foundation for more sophisticated training techniques, exercises and routines. Bodyshapers, in contrast, will use *Bodybuilding for Beginners* as their primary source of instruction.

The path you choose to take—bodyshaping or more serious bodybuilding—is entirely up to you. Regardless of the path you follow, however, I promise to give you the best available beginning- and intermediate-level bodybuilding information.

WHAT TO EXPECT

Bodybuilding training and nutritional practices are the quickest method available for enhancing physical appearance. Rachel McLish (twice Miss Olympia) summarized this for me: "There is a wide variety of types of exercise that a man or woman can use to shape and tone the body—running, swimming, aerobic exercise classes, calisthenics, stretching, participation in a sport, and so on. I've tried most forms of exercise, but none allowed me to change the appearance of my body as quickly or to such a markedly positive degree as bodybuilding. So, if you want to get the most out of the time you put into exercising, why not use the best form of exercise?"

Within only a week or two of training, you will notice improvements in the strength of your muscles. Within a month, your body will begin to look better, particularly if you have also begun to watch what you eat. Within a year, you can improve your physique to such an extent that friends and relatives who haven't seen you recently will be shocked by the change.

Dale Ruplinger (Mr. USA, American Middleweight Champion, and World Middleweight Champion) is a good example of such dramatic improvement. "Within a year of becoming a bodybuilder, I had totally reshaped my body," Dale told me following his Mr. USA win. "I knocked six inches off my waist and added more than three inches to my upper arm measurement within a year. My appearance changed so radically and quickly that my friends and relatives couldn't believe it. 'Dale, what have you *done* to yourself?' was a typical reaction. And this was invariably followed by myriad questions about how they could bring about a similar change."

Men are able to make much faster and more dramatic gains in muscle mass than women, because they secrete much greater amounts of the muscle-building hormone testosterone. Still, any woman can radically change the appearance of her body through weight training and diet.

Stacey Bentley (World Couples Champion) weighed 145 pounds at 5′1″ in height when she began working out. In a year her weight had dropped to 115 pounds, and within two years she weighed 105 pounds and had attained superb competitive bodybuilding condition. Remarkably, as her body slimmed down and grew stronger, Stacey's outlook on life also dramatically improved.

Underweight men and women can rapidly become excellent bodybuilders as well. Regardless of how bad a man's or woman's physical condition or appearance might be prior to adopting a bodybuilding lifestyle, incredibly positive changes can be wrought with only a year or two of training.

Lou Ferrigno (Mr. America, Mr. Universe) was 5′10″ tall and weighed only 135 pounds when he began bodybuilding at age 15. Louie was also painfully shy and introverted. Within five years of beginning serious training, his height had increased to 6′5″ and his body weight had grown to a muscular 265 pounds. As a bonus, Lou became an extrovert and eventually a film and television star.

"I owe everything to bodybuilding," Louie told me recently. "The training I did to build up my physique taught me how to work toward a goal with great intensity and total dedication. Bodybuilding taught me to be persistent, to work hard, to be self-reliant, and to look at myself objectively. More importantly, it dramatically improved my self-image, allowing me first to become a normal person after years as a shrinking violet and later to assert myself as an actor and a person."

As you have seen, it is possible to improve your appearance and self-image significantly through bodybuilding, regardless of gender. You can also make great improvements at any age. While the best ages for making bodybuilding gains are between 15 and

45, I know numerous youngsters under 15 and old-timers in their 60s, 70s, and even 80s who enjoy and benefit from their workouts.

Prior to about the age of 15 the human body isn't mature enough to make optimum gains in muscle mass; after the age of about 45 the body gains strength and muscle mass more and more slowly. Regardless of your age and sex, however, you can look forward to making astonishing improvements in the appearance of your physique. If you faithfully follow my instructions and don't miss any training sessions, I can *guarantee* that you'll improve quite rapidly.

BODYBUILDING POTENTIAL

The ultimate degree to which you can develop your physique—as well as the speed with which you can become a champion bodybuilder, given optimum training and diet—is governed by your genetic and environmental potential.

Champion bodybuilders are genetically gifted for the sport, and probably less than 5 percent of all men and women have the potential to become a Mr. or Miss Olympia. Perhaps another 5 percent will fail to have enough potential to become even city champions, but the remaining 90 percent of all men and women entering bodybuilding have the potential to become local, regional, and national champions.

Good genetic potential won't win a title for you if you don't train regularly and correctly or eat the right food, however. I've seen hundreds of very gifted bodybuilders squander their potential through improper or erratic training and poor diet. I've also seen many men and women with very poor potential reach the top through persistent and dedicated training. You alone determine how much of your potential development is actualized.

The most gifted men and women will have the following five physical attributes when in an untrained state:

1. higher-than-normal levels of strength and muscular development
2. a naturally low degree of body fat
3. relatively wide shoulders and a narrow waist-hip structure

4. relatively small knees, ankles, and wrists
5. above-average height (Although relatively short body-builders have won high-level titles, taller bodybuilders seem to have an advantage.)

Within a year of commencing regular training, three other factors of physical potential should become apparent. The best bodybuilders will discover that they make relatively fast gains in muscle mass and that no muscle groups fail to respond. Elite bodybuilders normally have trained muscles that are long and full, without long gaps between the muscle belly and a joint. As you become more experienced with bodybuilding, you will be able to evaluate all of these factors of physical potential quite easily.

These days a champion bodybuilder must also possess an above-average trained intellect (a factor largely subject to the person's environment while growing up). You must be intelligent and well-educated to understand the diverse scientific disciplines—anatomy, kinesiology, exercise physiology, psychology, and biochemistry—that can help you become a better body-builder. Champion professional bodybuilders must also possess well-developed business abilities if they intend to make a good living from the sport.

If you have been given poor genetic bodybuilding potential, you can still develop a fantastic physique *if* you dedicate yourself to your training. No bodybuilder has yet come close to actualizing his or her full potential, so you can look for better and better bodybuilders in the future. And, no matter how good you become, there will always be additional room for improvement. Perhaps you will be the first bodybuilder to reach his or her full physical potential.

PHYSIOLOGY OF BODYBUILDING

In bodybuilding training a muscle group is stressed with a resistance greater than it is normally accustomed to handling.

This resistance is applied either by using a weight heavier than the one lifted in a previous workout or by doing a greater number of repetitions (counts) with a set weight. In both cases the greater-than-normal resistance forces a muscle group to increase its hypertrophy (to grow in mass and strength).

There is debate in the scientific community about how the muscles actually increase in hypertrophy, but there is no doubt that muscles gradually increase in mass and strength as progressively heavier resistance is placed on them. Indeed, there is a linear relationship between the size of your muscles and their strength, leading to the first crucial axiom of bodybuilding: *the heavier the weights you use for a set number of repetitions in an exercise, the larger the muscles that move those weights.*

In Chapter 2, I will discuss how you can gradually and progressively increase the resistance you use in each exercise. This technique is called *progression,* and it is the practical means by which you coax your muscles to increase in hypertrophy.

ADVANTAGES AND DISADVANTAGES

Through my extensive experience with bodybuilding, I've discovered a few disadvantages that come with the territory. Each of these disadvantages can be neutralized, however, if you know how to combat them.

Following are the three primary disadvantages of bodybuilding, accompanied by the best methods of counteracting them:

1. *Bodybuilding training can be boring.* The repetitious nature of bodybuilding training can make it boring if you allow it to be. By frequently changing your training routines and carefully maintaining a high level of enthusiasm for your workouts, though, you can easily avoid boredom.

2. *It's difficult to find clothing that fits.* This drawback particularly applies to massively developed male bodybuilders. Can you imagine trying to buy an off-the-rack sportcoat and dress shirt to fit Lou Ferrigno's 21-inch neck, 58-inch chest, 34-inch waist, and 22-inch upper arms? The solution for many bodybuilders is to

purchase double-knit clothing. Or you can have some of your wardrobe tailored to fit your body. Tailoring is somewhat expensive, but any bodybuilder with clothing fit perfectly to his or her body measurements looks sensational. I think you'll find this to be more than worth the expense of tailoring.

3. *Food and food supplements can be expensive.* An average competitive bodybuilder will spend a minimum of $400 per year on protein supplements, vitamins, and minerals. And, because bodybuilders are quite physically active, they tend to eat more food than a normal person. The supplements might seem expensive, but you should look at them as health insurance. Primarily because bodybuilders follow healthy diets, they are seldom ill. So, the savings in medical bills more or less balances out the cost of food supplements. And, since bodybuilders waste little money on junk foods, they tend to spend little more than the average person on groceries.

Following are the six primary advantages of adopting a bodybuilding lifestyle:

1. *You will be much healthier than the average person.* There is also some evidence that following a healthy diet and exercising regularly contributes to longevity.

2. *It becomes easy to normalize your body weight.* Through proper diet and bodybuilding training, you will be able to gain muscle mass and/or lose body fat at will.

3. *Bodybuilding gives you valuable reserve strength.* This comes in handy if you're involved in a traffic accident or other life-threatening situation. For example, in my more foolish youth I fell headfirst off my motorcycle while traveling more than 100 mph down a beach and survived without a hint of injury.

4. *Bodybuilding exercises can be made specific to each muscle group.* Unlike in other forms of exercise, you can choose bodybuilding movements that stress single muscles in isolation from the rest of your body. This is particularly valuable when you have a body part that lags a bit behind the rest of your body, since you can choose several exercises with which to bomb the lagging muscle group unmercifully until it is again in proportion with the rest of your body.

5. *You can place an unlimited range of resistance on each*

muscle. With calisthenic exercises, you can use no greater resistance than your body weight, while bodybuilding allows you to use weights varying from as few as 2½ pounds in each hand to as many as 500–600 pounds. Lee Haney (American and World Champion), for example, does 6–8 repetitions with 500 pounds in the Bench Press. Laura Combes (American Champion) can use 400 pounds for several reps in a Deadlift. (Please refer to Chapter 3 for explanations and illustrations of these exercises if you are unfamiliar with them.)

6. *Bodybuilding develops positive personal qualities useful in all of life's endeavors.* As mentioned in the Lou Ferrigno quote earlier in this chapter, the bodybuilding lifestyle builds a strong character, an ability to work hard, persistence, concentration, a positive self-image, dedication, patience, the ability to set and reach goals, and a variety of other qualities useful in every human endeavor.

MUSCLE MYTHS

Even though the tremendous public exposure given to bodybuilding over the past decade has nearly dispelled most of the myths about bodybuilding, a few still survive. So that you won't have reservations about becoming a bodybuilder, here are the three most common muscle myths and the truth behind each:

1. *Training with weights will make you muscle-bound.* Actually, bodybuilders are far more flexible than the average person. Scientists began conducting experiments to test this more than 30 years ago, only to discover that weight training improves muscle and joint flexibility.

2. *All that muscle will turn to fat as soon as you stop working out.* Physiologically, it's impossible to convert muscle tissue to fat. Should you continue to eat as much food after you suspend training as you did while working out regularly, however, you *can* grow fat. The trick to staying lean when you stop working out—if you ever do—is either to reduce the amount of food you consume by 400–500 calories per day or to take up another form of exercise, such as running or cycling.

3. *You'll ruin your back lifting heavy weights.* Back injuries are

not unknown in bodybuilding circles, but they can be avoided almost totally if you follow correct warm-up practices (outlined in Chapter 2) and maintain correct biomechanical (body) positions in each exercise (Chapter 3).

YOUR LIFETIME GOALS

As long as you aspire to become a competitive bodybuilder, you must adhere to these three goals:

1. *Keep your body proportions in perfect balance.* This is the most important goal in bodybuilding, since contest judges look first for even proportions in each competitor. The keys to reaching this goal are to avoid favoring certain body parts and to bomb all lagging muscle groups unmercifully until they are up to par.

2. *Maintain a low percentage of body fat.* Every bodybuilder must have a minimum of body fat when onstage competing, and it's difficult to rid your body of accumulated fat. Therefore, it's a good practice to follow a low-calorie diet in the off-season to keep your body from accumulating useless fat.

3. *Train first for muscle quality.* This goal is actually a combination of the preceding two, but it merits mention. Far too many upcoming bodybuilders are preoccupied with adding mass to their bodies at the expense of maintaining good proportions and muscle quality. In competitive bodybuilding bigger isn't necessarily better. Frank Zane has frequently proven this by defeating men who outweigh him by 30–40 pounds. If you train to achieve perfect proportions and superior muscle quality, mass will come gradually and you will always outscore a larger bodybuilder with poor proportions and/or lesser muscle quality.

The physical qualities of a champion bodybuilder are balanced body proportions, muscularity (an absence of body fat), good symmetry (the shape of the muscles), and a high degree of muscle mass. Proportional balance is the most important of these qualities and muscle mass the least important.

THE PUMP

Bodybuilders are invariably hooked on the pleasant sensation of a good muscle pump, the tight, blood-congested feeling in a muscle when it has been trained hard. A pump feels great, and it's an infallible sign that you have worked a muscle optimally. You will soon seek a good pump in every workout, because it *is* such a good feeling and an unerring sign of impending muscle growth. And once you have achieved a good pump, you'll be after it for life!

2

Essential Techniques

You must master the basic techniques and information presented in this chapter in order to have safe and productive workouts. In fact, you could profit from reading this material several times, because its information will give you a solid foundation on which to build your physique workout by workout over the next few years.

BASIC TERMINOLOGY

There are several terms in common use in bodybuilding circles. You should understand each of them before training in a public gym or reading additional bodybuilding books and magazines.

An *exercise* is each individual movement performed, such as a Sit-Up or Bench Press. *Exercise* and *movement* are used interchangeably.

A *repetition,* or *rep,* is each complete cycle of an exercise, such as sitting erect and then allowing your torso to return to a position on the floor in a Sit-Up. A *set* is a distinct group of repetitions (usually in the range of 6–12) followed by a *rest interval* of 60–70 seconds between sets. You will usually perform two or more sets of each exercise.

A *routine* is the entire grouping of exercises, sets, and reps done in one *training session* or *workout*. A routine is often called a *program* or *training schedule*.

You will encounter other unfamiliar terms as you continue to learn more about bodybuilding. Many of them will be defined in the glossary at the back of this book. The meaning of any others can be deduced by studying the context in which they are used. With a little practice you will soon be speaking "bodybuildingese" with the best bodybuilders you encounter.

EQUIPMENT ORIENTATION

There will also be an array of unfamiliar bodybuilding equipment in any gym or health spa you enter. The most basic piece of equipment is a *barbell*. A barbell consists of a metal *bar* four to six feet long, over which a hollow metal tube called a *sleeve* is fitted to allow the weight to revolve more easily in your hands. Grooves called *knurlings* are cut into the sleeve to assist a bodybuilder's grip when his or her hands are sweaty.

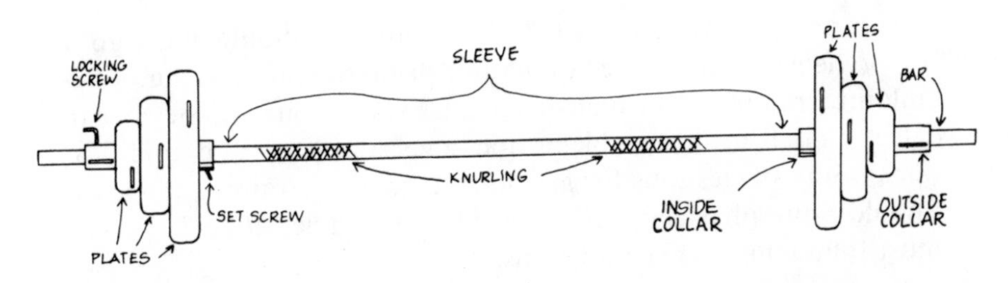

Collars are cylindrical metal clamps that hold *plates* (metal or concrete-filled vinyl discs) on the bar. There are usually *inside collars* and *outside collars* that keep the plates from moving along the bar. *Set screws* are threaded through the collars to clamp them firmly against the bar.

An *exercise barbell* is much less expensive than an *Olympic barbell,* which is specially machined for use in weightlifting competitions and heavy bodybuilding training. Exercise barbells are used to do lighter exercises.

Large gyms have a range of *fixed barbells* with the plates welded permanently in place. The weight of each fixed barbell and dumbbell is painted on its plates. A good range of fixed weights saves the considerable time you would spend loading and unloading adjustable barbells and dumbbells.

Dumbbells are shorter versions of barbells intended for use in one hand. Dumbbells have the same characteristics and terminology as barbells. Most dumbbell exercises affect the upper body muscles.

A wide variety of *benches, pulleys,* and other apparatus exist for use with *free weights* (barbells, dumbbells, and loose plates). The names and functions of these pieces of equipment will be obvious when you read the exercise descriptions in Chapter 3.

As you gain experience, you will encounter many resistance machines, such as those manufactured by Nautilus Sports/Medical Industries and Universal Gyms. I will discuss the use of exercise machines in Chapter 5.

PHYSICAL EXAMS

Any man or woman past high school age should undergo a comprehensive physical examination prior to commencing bodybuilding training. Through such an exam, your physician can detect hidden health problems and suggest appropriate modifications of my suggestions for gradually increasing training intensity. Should your physician give you different advice than I do, you must follow his or her directions.

If you are over 35, it's a good practice to have a stress-test electrocardiogram. Past 40, a stress-test EKG is essential.

PROGRESSION

As mentioned, progressive increases in training intensity are at the heart of bodybuilding training. Intensity is increased in three ways:

1. Increase the amount of weight you handle for a given number of repetitions in an exercise.

2. Increase the number of reps you do with a set weight in an exercise.

3. Decrease the rest intervals between sets of an exercise done with a consistent weight and number of reps.

Competitive bodybuilders use the third method of augmenting training intensity, but only for a few weeks prior to a competition. More commonly, bodybuilders increase intensity by progressively increasing the weight and reps in a movement.

With the most fundamental method of progression, you will gradually increase the number of reps from a "lower guide number" to an "upper guide number," then increase the weight used by 5–10 pounds and drop your reps back to the lower guide number. Work up again to the upper guide number to repeat the procedure.

Flip ahead to one of the routines listed in Chapter 4 under the "Reps" column, and you'll see a range of repetitions listed (e.g., 8–12). In this case, 8 is the lower guide number and 12 is the upper number. Assuming you are doing one set of 8–12 reps on the Bench Press, here is a sample progression of weight and reps over a four-week period (40 × 8 is shorthand for *40 pounds for eight reps*):

	Monday	**Wednesday**	**Friday**
Week 1	40 × 8	40 × 9	40 × 10
Week 2	40 × 11	40 × 12	45 × 8
Week 3	45 × 9	45 × 10	45 × 11
Week 4	45 × 12	50 × 8	50 × 9

You'll usually be able to add one or two new reps during each workout, though occasionally on a "down" day you won't be able to add a rep. Don't let this worry you, because on an "up" day you'll be able to add several repetitions.

Men can normally add 5–10 pounds to upper body exercises and 10–20 pounds to leg movements whenever they reach an upper guide number. Women can usually add 2½–5 pounds to upper body exercises and 5–10 pounds to leg movements. Individual strength levels vary widely, however, so you may appropriately add more or less than these figures each time.

You will usually do two or three sets of each exercise, which involves reaching the upper guide number on each set before adding weight. Here's a sample four-week progression for three sets of 8–12 reps in the Barbell Bent Rowing movement:

	Monday	Wednesday	Friday
Week 1	60 × 8	60 × 10	60 × 11
	60 × 8	60 × 9	60 × 10
	60 × 8	60 × 8	60 × 9
Week 2	60 × 12	60 × 12	60 × 12
	60 × 12	60 × 12	60 × 12
	60 × 10	60 × 11	60 × 12
Week 3	65 × 9	65 × 11	65 × 12
	65 × 8	65 × 10	65 × 10
	65 × 8	65 × 9	65 × 10
Week 4	65 × 11	65 × 12	65 × 12
	65 × 10	65 × 11	65 × 12
	65 × 10	65 × 10	65 × 11

With this method of gradual progression, you'll be able to add weight to all of your exercises *ad infinitum*. With each exercise poundage increase, your muscles will become a bit larger and stronger.

TRAINING TEMPO

The speed with which you move a barbell or dumbbell during an exercise and the length of time you rest between sets are two important training tempo factors. The weight should be raised and lowered fairly slowly so that momentum can't rob your muscles of any resistance they should be feeling. You should also lower the weight a bit more slowly than you raise it, because scientists have determined that the negative (downward) cycle of a movement has great potential for developing strength and muscle mass.

Take two or three seconds to raise the weight slowly, under full control, and lower it over a three- or four-second period. Using this as a starting point, experiment with the tempo at which you raise and lower the weight, aiming for a full-range movement in which you can *feel* the weight along the full positive (upward) and negative phases of each repetition.

As an experienced bodybuilder, you will vary the length of rest intervals between sets according to the phase of your training (either off-season or precontest). For now, however, I would suggest that you rest for 60–70 seconds between each set, a rest interval that will allow your working muscles to recuperate sufficiently to do justice to the next set. It is also a short enough interval to keep your body warm to avoid injury.

Later you'll learn to vary the length of your rest intervals according to workout goals. When training for mass and power in the off-season, you will probably rest for up to two minutes between sets. Prior to a competition, when hardening up and polishing your development, you might rest for as few as 15–20 seconds between sets.

TRAINING FREQUENCY

When you have optimally trained a muscle you must give it 48–72 hours of rest before bombing it again. A muscle doesn't grow in mass and strength as you train it, but during the two or three days of rest following a workout. So, if you try to work a muscle group every day, it is unable to recuperate and grow.

Initially, you should work out on three nonconsecutive days per week, a scheme that allows you two days of rest following two of your workouts and three rest days after the other. Most commonly, novice bodybuilders will train on Mondays, Wednesdays, and Fridays, a pattern that leaves weekends free for other recreational activities. Any other three nonconsecutive training days each week are also acceptable.

After 10–12 weeks of preparatory training you can move up to working out four days per week on a split routine. In this case you will train half of your major muscle groups on Mondays and Thursdays, the other half on Tuesdays and Fridays, and your calves and abs all four days. With a split routine, half of your body rests while the other half is trained. You will become more familiar with a split routine in Chapter 4.

WHEN TO WORK OUT

As long as you can find a consistent time of day at which to train, it matters little what specific hour you choose. For most of the 20 years during which he dominated the NABBA Mr. Universe competition, Bill Pearl trained at 5:30 in the morning, so his workout would be finished before he opened his gym for business. World Grand Prix Champion Boyer Coe began training at well after midnight when he was both going to college and running a new business. There was no other time at which he could train, so Boyer made do excellently with his middle-of-the-night workouts.

Even though numerous champion bodybuilders train at odd hours of the day, I've noticed three peak periods during which the largest numbers of bodybuilders work out at Gold's Gym. A number of the best pro bodybuilders—such as Tom Platz—like to train between 10:00 a.m. and noon. Another big wave hits the gym about 3:30 or 4:00 p.m. when school lets out, and the largest number of bodybuilders arrives at Gold's to train at about 5:30 when work has concluded for the day.

WHERE TO TRAIN

Most champion bodybuilders train in a large, well-equipped commercial gym such as Gold's or the World Gym, both located in southern California. An upcoming champ can improve faster when inspired to train harder by the sport's elite athletes and when the best bodybuilders are available to give advice. And these are the primary reasons that so many good young bodybuilders move to California to train.

Still, many great bodybuilders win major championships while training in home gyms, and a majority of the champs who work out at big gyms began training at home in a garage or basement. Dr. Franco Columbu trained almost exclusively in his garage when preparing to win his first Mr. Olympia title. Lou Ferrigno and Rachel McLish did their initial workouts at home before moving on to commercial gyms. And Jean LeBlanc (multiple Canadian Champion) lives in a small town in New Brunswick, where he trains exclusively in his well-equipped basement gym.

So, if you are training at home with your own barbell and dumbbell set, you can make it to the top. I would suggest, however, that you gradually add to your stock of extra barbell plates and other apparatus so that you have a decently equipped home gym in which to train. All of the companies listed in Chapter 7 sell home gym equipment, and you can send for their brochures and catalogs.

Also, once you begin to develop an outstanding physique, you need not immediately move to Los Angeles. Champion bodybuilders live and train all over the United States, Canada, and the rest of the world. As an example, the four outstanding winners of the NPC National Championships in 1982 lived far from California. James Gaubert (Lightweight Champion) is from Louisiana, Dale Ruplinger (Middleweight) is from Iowa, Moses Maldonado (Light-Heavyweight) is from New York City, and Lee Haney (Heavyweight) hails from South Carolina.

Regardless of where you train, you can be a winner if you are persistent, consistent in your workouts, dedicated, and willing to give 100 percent effort 100 percent of the time.

WORKOUT ATTIRE

The training clothing worn by champion bodybuilders varies widely. Chris Dickerson (Mr. Olympia) invariably wears a full sweat suit; Rachel McLish prefers shorts, dance tights, and a leotard; many others wear only shorts or shorts and a tank top. Robby Robinson (American and World Champion) used to wear shorts and a ragged old T-shirt held together with myriad knots. Robby changed to new training attire only when a fan purchased the historic shirt for $100.

There are two key points to ponder when choosing what to wear for a workout: (1) Be sure the clothing is loose fitting or elastic enough to allow free movement of your limbs over an exaggerated range of motion. (2) Your workout clothing must be warm enough to keep your body from cooling off during a workout and becoming susceptible to injury.

Basic training attire should consist of shorts and a T-shirt or tank top. An athletic supporter or bra is optional. Over the shorts and shirt you can wear warm-up pants and/or a jacket if it's cool in the gym. Many women wear tights under their shorts when it's a bit cold. The key to dressing warmly in cold weather is to wear several thin layers of clothing rather than one thick layer. Light layers trap insulating pockets of air, which keep you very comfortable.

Although I see many bodybuilders training barefoot, it's wise to wear running shoes during a workout. The tread on these shoes helps your feet adhere to a toe block when you do calf exercises. And the arch support built into all running shoes protects the arches of your feet from compression injuries when you are training with very heavy poundages. Add a pair of thick sweat socks, and you're ready for a great workout.

WEIGHTLIFTING BELTS

You should wear a wide leather weightlifting belt cinched around your waist when you do heavy back exercises (e.g., Barbell Bent Rowing and Deadlifts), Squats, and overhead exercises (e.g., Military Presses). A weightlifting belt protects your lower back from injury when using heavy poundages in the exercises just mentioned. These belts cost $20–$30, and they are available at sporting goods stores and through ads in bodybuilding magazines.

STARTING POUNDAGES

In Chapter 4 I've listed several novice-level bodybuilding routines. If you haven't been working out with weights, you won't know how to choose an appropriate starting poundage for each listed exercise. Therefore, I have suggested starting weights for both men (see the column marked "% Men") and women ("% Women").

The columns suggesting starting weights have numbers referring to a percentage of your body weight. Thus, if you are a man weighing 150 pounds and are to use 50% of your body weight in a particular movement, you should load the bar up to 75 pounds. As you load the bar, however, be sure to include the weight of the bar itself, not merely that of the plates, in your poundage calculation.

Always round *down* to the nearest five-pound increment when calculating a starting poundage. As an example, if you are a woman weighing 120 pounds and you're using 30 percent of your body weight, load the bar to 35 pounds ($120 \times 0.30 = 36$, rounded down to 35).

I have estimated starting poundages according to strength levels of average men and women, as I have observed them over the years. If you have been physically active or you are naturally stronger, you may find these weights too light. Or, if you've been sedentary or you are significantly overweight, the poundages might feel too heavy. Adjust the weights upward or downward according to how they feel to you in your first workout.

Once you have a few weeks of steady training under your belt, you'll have no problem estimating your starting poundages for exercises in future programs. Therefore, I have recommended starting weights only for the initial training routine.

REPETITION RANGES

Over a period of time, you will notice that your body responds better to certain ranges of repetitions. As an example, for pressing movements (Bench Presses, Inclines, Militaries), you will probably discover that moderately low reps (6–10) will work best.

Thighs often require higher reps (10–15), and calves need even higher reps (15–20). The abdominals respond to a wide range of repetitions (15–100), and the rest of the body normally responds best to medium reps (8–12).

If you are training for mass and power in an off-season cycle, you will usually get good results with lower reps (4–6), while in a hardening phase you'll need to do higher repetitions (10–15) on most exercises. Overall, the number of reps you do for each body part will be highly individual, and you'll need to determine the rep schemes you use through systematic experimentation and careful observation.

EXERCISE FORM

In Chapter 5, I will explain how to cheat in your method of doing an exercise, but at the very beginning level it's essential that you maintain strict exercise form. Strict form involves moving a weight over the full range of motion prescribed for an exercise, plus moving only the part(s) of the body that should be moved in the exercise.

The most common types of cheating involve bending the back and jerking the knees to help the weight up in an exercise. Since cheating robs your muscles of much of the resistance they should feel, you must keep your exercise form very strict during the first few months of bodybuilding training.

BREATHING PATTERNS

Students in my beginning weight training and bodybuilding classes seemed to ask more questions about how to breathe while working out than about any other aspect of pumping iron. Essentially, as long as you don't hold your breath during an exercise, you're doing fine. Holding your breath as you exert yourself can be dangerous, since it could cause you to pass out. If you fainted while doing Bench Presses with a very heavy weight, you could be seriously injured, even killed.

If you feel that you need a rule for breathing during an

exercise, breathe in during the relaxation phase of a movement (usually as you lower the weight) and out as you exert. Usually, you'll find natural points in a movement when it's most comfortable to breathe in or out, however. As long as you *do* breathe in and out, you needn't worry about when to breathe during a set.

SLEEP AND REST

One of the most vital requisites to muscle growth—along with hard training and proper diet—is complete muscle and body recuperation between workouts. And the requisites to full recuperation are enough sleep and rest.

The average person requires eight hours of sleep each night, but this amount varies widely from individual to individual. Some champion bodybuilders require six or fewer hours of sleep each night, while others need more than 10 hours. Regardless of the amount of time you require for sleep, be sure to get enough so you feel fully rested each morning.

Once you have been training with weights for a few weeks, you will find that you fall asleep much more easily and sleep more deeply. The hard work of bodybuilding training is very conducive to healthy sleep.

You should also try to rest periodically during the day, particularly if you have a physically demanding job. A short nap each day would be best, but merely taking 10–15 minutes to relax mentally and physically will do a lot to promote faster muscle growth.

THE MIND IN BODYBUILDING

Champion bodybuilders have mastered the use of mind power to further their bodybuilding efforts. You will learn a wide variety of advanced mental techniques as you continue your bodybuilding, but there are three techniques that you should immediately attempt to master.

The first technique—and one that is central to many philosophies of life—is positive thinking. There are millions of negative people in the world, and many of them will do their best to cut your legs from under you. Don't allow yourself to be dragged down to their level, or you'll never succeed as a competitive bodybuilder.

Bodybuilders are very positive men and women, so you must always try to think positively, casting out negative thoughts whenever they intrude on your thinking. Through bodybuilding you can and *will* excel, so there is no reason to fear failure.

Second, you must soon learn to concentrate on the working muscles, during each repetition of an exercise. Focus your mind on your biceps as you do a Barbell Curl, trying to visualize the muscles strongly contracting and extending during every repetition. Do this for every exercise—using a mirror at first to visually monitor your working muscles—and you'll soon master the art of concentration. Then your muscles will have a chance to grow at an optimum rate.

Your third mental bodybuilding technique is to regularly set and reach goals in your training poundages and muscular development. You should set both long-term and short-term goals. Long-term goals can be established at one-year intervals, then broken down into more realistic one-month short-term goals.

Let's say that you set a yearly goal of doing your Bench Presses or Deadlifts with 50 additional pounds. It's mind-boggling to think of handling so much more a year from now, isn't it? In order for your mind to handle the task a little more easily, you can aim for handling only five more pounds in a month's time. Five pounds isn't that much, but 12 months of gaining a mere five pounds amounts to a yearly gain of 60 pounds, not 50!

Regularly setting and achieving realistic goals will push your physique inexorably toward the top, step by step over the years. Add positive thinking and concentration to good goal setting, and you'll make much better progress through increased mind power.

WORKOUT BREAK-IN

Bodybuilding training is very heavy muscular exercise, so it's essential that you gradually break in to full-scale training in order to avoid sore muscles. Begin this break-in with one set of each recommended exercise in the initial routine in Chapter 4 for the first week. During your second week of training, do two sets of each movement for which multiple sets are recommended. At the beginning of your third week of training you can safely perform the full routine.

Even when following this progressive break-in, you may still experience moderate muscle soreness. In my experience the best remedy is a long, hot bath.

WARM-UPS

It has been scientifically demonstrated that a proper warm-up both prevents weight training injuries and makes a bodybuilding workout more productive. Therefore, you should always spend 5–10 minutes warming up before every workout.

A good warm-up should commence with two or three minutes of rope skipping or jogging in place. Follow this with four or five minutes of calisthenics and stretching exercises. This warm-up should bring you to the point where your pulse rate is higher and you have begun to perspire a bit. Only then are you ready to hit the iron.

Later, when you are using much heavier weights, you can add a high-repetition set of Bench Presses, Barbell Bent Rows, and Squats to your warm-up. This extra resistance warm-up will further prepare your muscles for the much heavier loads that might injure a muscle or joint that hasn't had such an extensive warm-up.

SAFETY RULES

If commonly accepted safety procedures are not followed, serious injuries—even death—can occur. I have acted as an expert consultant in several lawsuits stemming from weight training injuries, so I'm not exaggerating the dangers of training without a knowledge of correct safety procedures in a bodybuilding setting.

Fortunately, bodybuilding training can be made totally safe if you are careful to follow these 12 sensible safety rules:

1. Use spotters standing by to rescue you if you fail to complete a repetition of a heavy lift.
2. Never train alone.
3. Use catch racks on Bench Press benches and Squat stands.
4. Always use collars on barbells.
5. Don't hold your breath while lifting a weight.
6. Practice good gym housekeeping, picking up all loose weights and placing them in proper racks and storage areas.
7. Train under competent supervision.
8. Don't train in an overcrowded gym.
9. Warm up thoroughly before each workout.
10. Use proper biomechanical (body) positions when doing all exercises.
11. Use a weightlifting belt when doing heavy Squats, back exercises, and overhead lifts.
12. Acquire as much knowledge about bodybuilding as possible through books, magazines, and seminars.

RECORD KEEPING

Virtually all champion bodybuilders recommend keeping good written records of their training, diet, and other factors that have a bearing on their progress. Arnold Schwarzenegger always says in his training seminars, "Write it down!" And Rachel McLish revealed, "Keeping a detailed diary is the best way to make good sense of the confusing array of exercises and techniques confronting all bodybuilders."

You can keep your records in a notebook or use an excellent logbook that we produced at *Muscle & Fitness* magazine and had published by Contemporary Books. It's called the *Muscle & Fitness Training Diary,* and it has plenty of space for diary notes, plus informative training tips and inspirational photos. Look for it in all bookstores.

Keeping a detailed record of exercises, sets, and reps makes you aware of what regimen works best for you.

At a minimum, you should record the date of each workout, plus the exercises, sets, weights, and reps that you do. Using the shorthand suggested in the section on progression, you can make an entry like this:

Bench Press: 75 × 10 × 10 × 9

In the foregoing example, you have done two sets of 10 and one set of nine reps in the Bench Press with 75 pounds.

You can also record your body weight and measurements at one-month intervals. And many bodybuilders (such as Andreas Cahling) record every morsel of food they consume each day. You can even write down how much you sleep, your mood prior to each workout, and a wide variety of other variables that might have an effect on each workout.

With a good training diary, you can look back and determine when you had growth spurts and what led to these periods of accelerated growth. And this invaluable knowledge can ultimately help you discover which training techniques and nutritional practices will lead you to the fastest muscle gains.

3

Your Exercises

More than 40 basic muscle-building exercises are fully described and illustrated in this chapter. You will use all of them periodically as long as you continue your bodybuilding workouts, so it's essential that you learn to do them correctly from the beginning.

You can learn each new movement without additional coaching by following these four steps:

1. Read the description.
2. Reread the description while reviewing the exercise photos accompanying the text of this chapter.
3. Use a broomstick to run through the exercise without a weight.
4. Do the exercise with a light weight, slowly working it into your routine using heavier and heavier poundages.

The exercises presented in the balance of this chapter are divided into groupings for each major muscle area of the body, except the neck. Most bodybuilders have found that the neck

Squat—start.

muscles grow rapidly enough merely from doing movements for the shoulders, upper chest, and upper back.

THIGH EXERCISES

Squats

The *Squat* is considered the best basic exercise for thigh development. It also places stress on the back muscles and helps make your metabolism anabolic so you can gain muscle all over your body.

Squat—finish.

Place a barbell across your shoulders and behind your neck and balance it in place by grasping the barbell bar. If the weight hurts your neck, wrap the bar with a towel. Place your feet at about shoulder width, your toes pointed slightly outward. Keeping your eyes focused on a point at shoulder height, with your torso erect, slowly bend your knees and sink into a full squatting position. Without bouncing at the bottom, slowly return to the starting point. If you have difficulty with your balance in the bottom position of the movement, you can stand with your heels on a two-by-four-inch block of wood as you do the exercise.

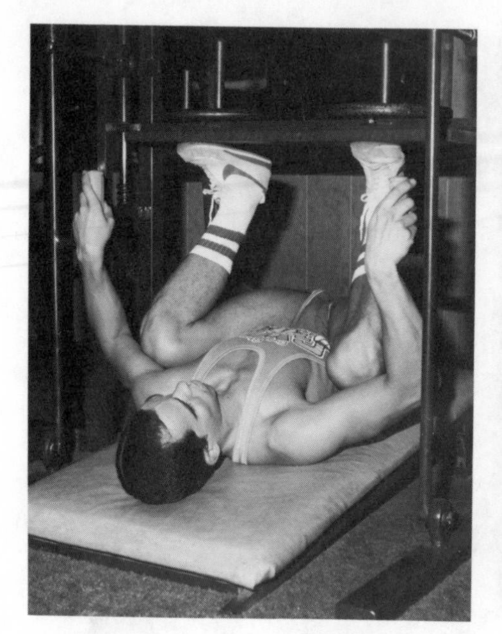

Leg Press—start, left; finish, right.

Leg Presses

A *Leg Press* exercise is equivalent to a Squat, except that it doesn't involve the back muscles. Lie on the padded board under the sliding platform of a leg press machine. Your hips should be placed at the upper end of the angled pad directly beneath the platform. Position your feet at shoulder width on the platform and straighten your legs. Release the platform by pulling or rotating the machine's stop bars. Slowly bend your legs fully, making sure your knees spread apart and don't contact your chest in the low position. Straighten your legs and return the platform to the starting point. Be sure to lock the stop bars at the end of your set. In some gyms you will see a Universal or Nautilus leg press machine, both of which allow you to sit erect as you do the movement.

Lunge—start, left; finish, right.

Lunges

Bodybuilders do the *Lunge* to stress the muscles of their thighs, buttocks, and hips. Begin the exercise in the same starting position as for Squats, except without your heels on a block of wood. Keeping your right leg only slightly bent, step forward 2½–3 feet with your left foot. Then slowly bend your left leg as fully as possible while keeping your torso erect. At the bottom point of the movement your right knee should be four to six inches from the floor and your left knee about six inches in front of your left ankle. Push yourself back to the starting point and repeat the movement with your right foot forward. Alternate forward legs for the required number of reps, counting one repetition each time both feet have been forward.

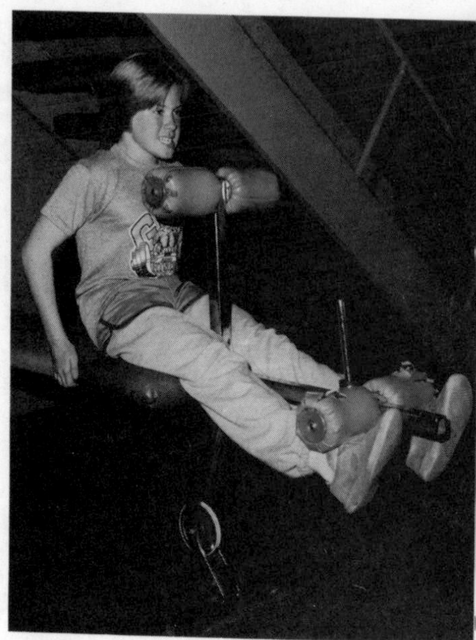

Leg Extensions—start, left; finish, right.

Leg Extensions

The *Leg Extension* is a good exercise for isolating stress on your frontal thigh muscles. Sit on the padded surface of a leg extension machine with the backs of your knees against the edge of the pad. Hook your insteps under the lower set of roller pads (if there are two sets) and grasp the edges of the bench or the handles provided to steady your body in position during the movement. From this starting position, slowly straighten your legs, pause for a moment with them fully straight, then allow the weight of the machine to return your legs slowly to the starting point.

Leg Curls

You can do the *Leg Curl* exercise to directly stress the hamstring muscles at the backs of your legs. Lie facedown on the

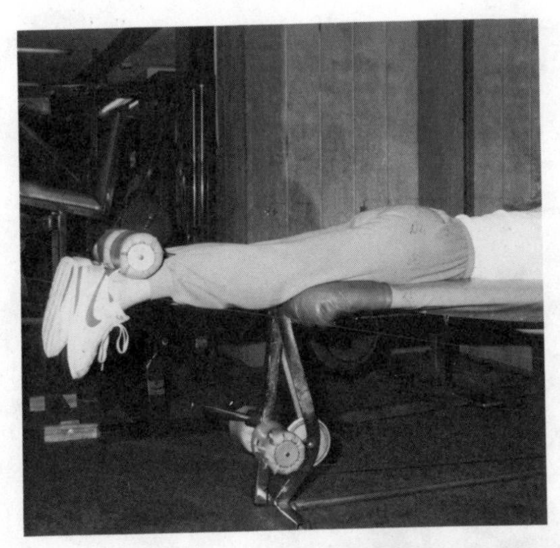

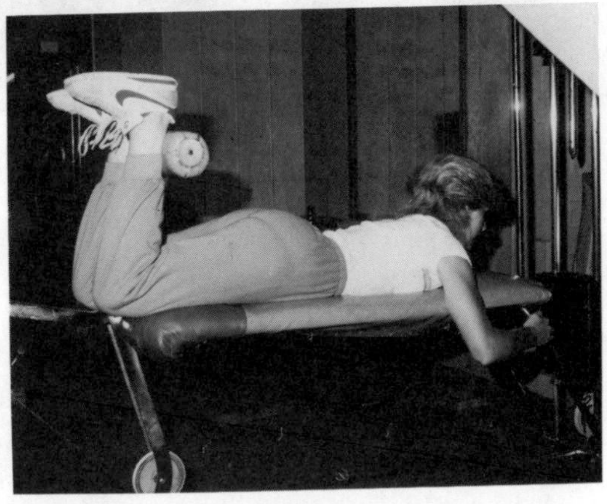

Leg Curl—start, top; finish, bottom.

padded surface of the machine, your knees near the edge of the pad. Hook your heels under the upper set of roller pads (if there are two sets) and grasp the edges of the bench or the handles provided to steady your body in position during the movement. From this starting position, slowly bend your legs as fully as possible, pause for a moment with them fully bent, and allow the weight of the machine to return your legs slowly to a straight position. Be sure to keep your hips in contact with the machine's padded surface at all times.

Upright Rowing—start, left; finish, right.

BACK EXERCISES

Upright Rowing

The *Upright Rowing* exercise is excellent for building up the trapezius and deltoid muscles. It also places stress on the biceps and forearms. Take a narrow overgrip in the middle of a barbell (there should be about six inches of space between your index fingers). Stand erect with your feet set at shoulder width and your arms hanging straight down at your sides. (When you have an overgrip on a barbell in this position your palms will be facing your body.) Slowly pull the barbell up the front of your body, keeping it no more than two or three inches away from your torso, until it touches the underside of your chin. As you pull the bar upward you should be careful to keep your elbows above the level of your hands. You should be particularly careful of this elbow placement at the top point of the movement. Slowly lower the barbell back to the starting point.

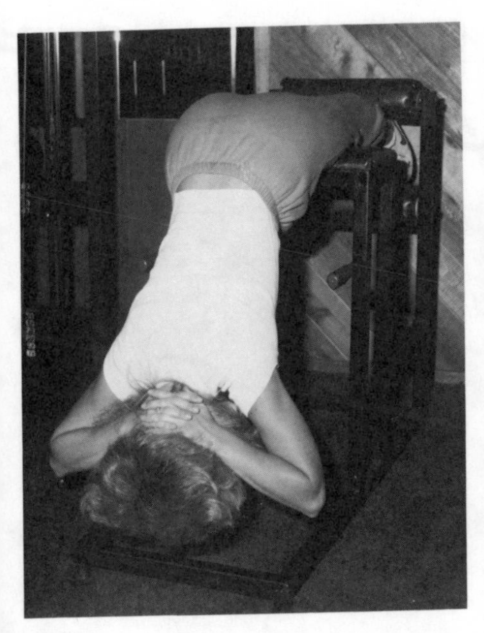

Hyperextension—start, left; finish, right.

Hyperextensions

The *Hyperextension* exercise directly stresses the powerful lower back muscles and places secondary emphasis on the hamstring muscles. Stand between the two pads of a hyperextension bench, facing the larger pad. Lean forward and place your pelvis across that pad, allowing your heels to rest against the underside of the smaller pad behind yourself. Lean even farther forward, flexing your hips at the waist so your torso hangs directly downward as illustrated. Place your hands behind your head. Slowly arch your back to move your torso upward until it is above an imaginary line drawn parallel to the floor. Return to the starting point. If you need more resistance on this exercise, simply hold a loose barbell plate behind your head. If no hyperextension bench is available, you can improvise by lying with your legs across a high bench or table. A training partner then lies across your legs to restrain your body during the movement.

Deadlift—start, left; finish, right.

Deadlifts

Bodybuilders do the *Deadlift* to muscle up their lower back, hips, and thighs. Deadlifts also stress the upper back and forearm muscles to a degree. Stand up to a loaded barbell, with your shins almost touching the bar. Bend over and take an overgrip on the bar with your hands set a little wider than your shoulders on each side. Dip your hips until they are below the level of your shoulders and above your knees. Flatten your back, keep your head up, and keep your arms straight throughout the movement. This starting position is fairly complicated, so carefully analyze the photo of this position. From the starting point, slowly straighten first your legs, then your back, to stand erect with the barbell across your thighs. Pull your shoulders back at the top point of the movement. Slowly lower the barbell back to the starting point by first bending your back slightly, then bending your legs, to bring the bar to rest gently on the floor.

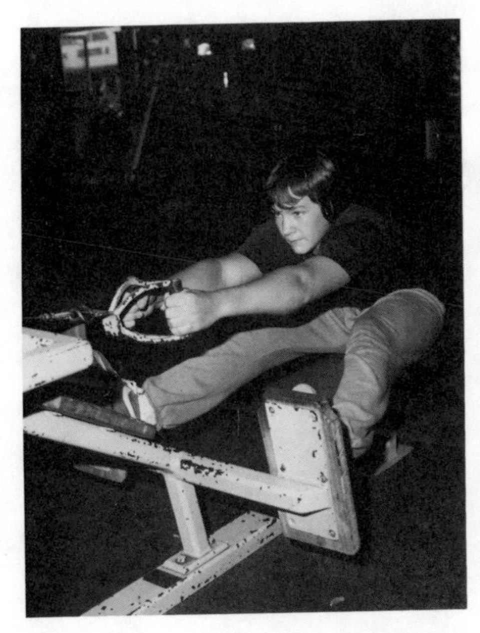

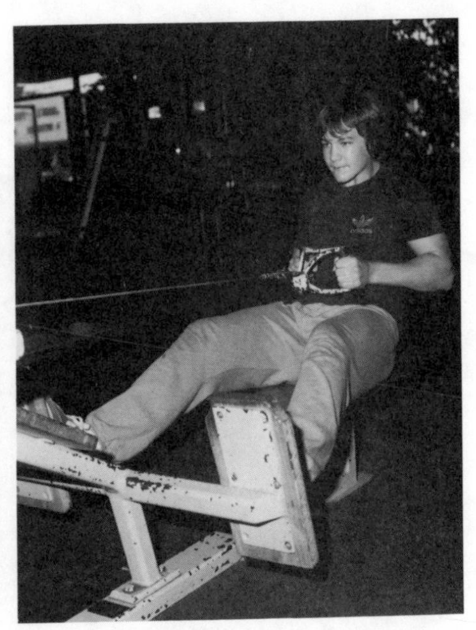

Seated Pulley Rowing—start, left; finish, right.

Seated Pulley Rowing

The *Seated Pulley Rowing* exercise builds both width and thickness in the latissimus dorsi muscles of the upper back. Grasp a handle that places your hands close together in a parallel grip. Place the arches of your feet against the restraining bar of the machine's seat and sit back. Keeping your legs slightly bent throughout the movement, lean your torso forward over your thighs and fully straighten your arms to stretch your upper back muscles. You can stretch your lats even more completely by lowering your head between your arms. From this starting position, slowly pull the handle in to touch your upper abdomen. You should simultaneously bring your torso erect and arch your back. Without arching your back on lat movements, you can't fully contract the muscle group. Reverse the pulling procedure to return to the starting point.

Barbell Bent Rowing—start, left; finish, right.

Barbell Bent Rowing

Barbell Bent Rowing is similar to Seated Pulley Rowing, except that it builds more thickness than width in the lats. Place your feet at about shoulder width and bend over at the waist until your torso is parallel to the floor. As with Pulley Rows, you must keep your legs slightly bent during the movement to remove undue stress from your lower back. Take a shoulder-width overgrip on a barbell and fully straighten your arms to stretch your lats. If you can't do this without letting the barbell plates touch the floor, stand on a thick block of wood. Keeping your torso as motionless as possible, slowly pull the weight up to touch your lower rib cage, being sure that your upper arms travel outward at about 45-degree angles from your torso. Slowly lower the weight back to the starting position.

Dumbbell Bent Rowing—start, left; finish, right.

Dumbbell Bent Rowing

You can use a single dumbbell for *Dumbbell Bent Rowing*, which also adds thickness to your lats. Stand with your left side next to a flat exercise bench. Bend over at the waist so your torso is parallel to the floor and place your left hand on the bench to brace your body. Your left leg should be set a little forward and bent, and your right leg should be extended to the rear and fairly straight. Grasp a dumbbell in your right hand and straighten your arm to stretch the muscles on the right side of your upper back. From this position, slowly pull the dumbbell up to touch the side of your rib cage. Lower the weight back to the starting point.

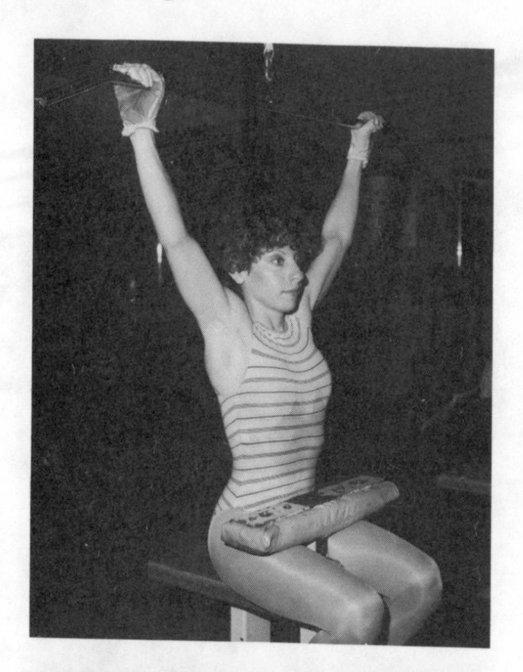

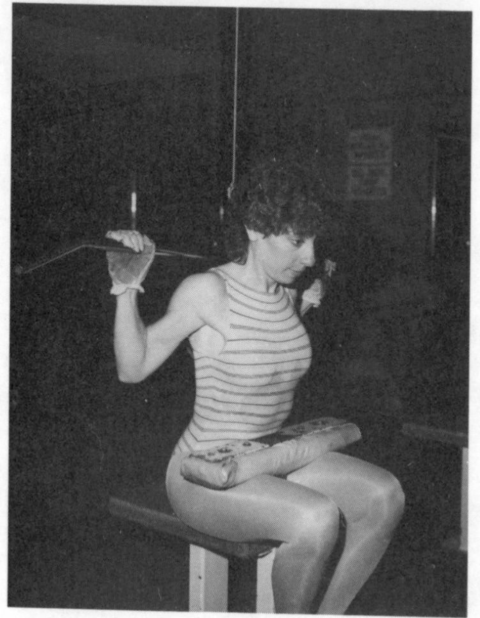

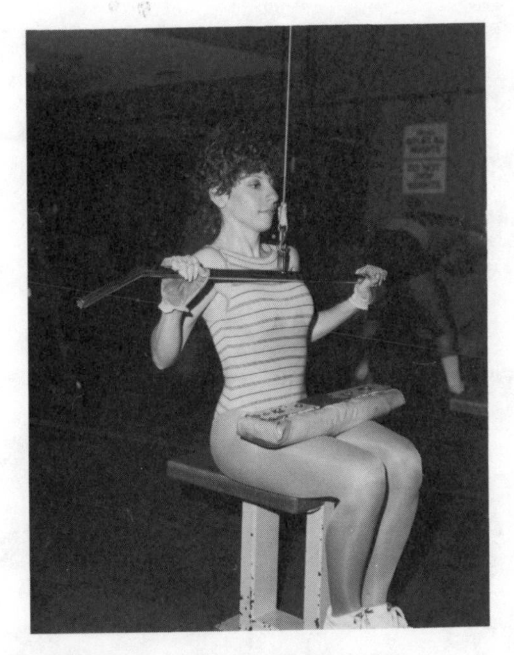

Lat Pulldown—start, top left; finish (behind neck), bottom left; and finish (in front of neck), above.

Lat Pulldowns

Lat Pulldowns add width to your latissimus dorsi muscles. Take an overgrip on the lat bar so your hands are set four to six inches wider than your shoulders on each side. Either sit or kneel directly beneath the pulley and fully straighten your arms. Many lat machines have a seat and crossbar under which you can wedge your knees to restrain your body during the exercise. From this starting position, slowly pull the bar down to touch the back of your neck. Alternatively, you can pull the bar down in front of your face to touch your upper chest, or you can alternate reps to the front and back of your neck. Slowly return the bar to the starting position and repeat the movement.

Barbell Bench Press—start.

CHEST EXERCISES

Barbell Bench Presses

The *Barbell Bench Press* is the most basic chest movement. It strongly stresses the pectorals, frontal deltoids, and triceps. Lie back on a flat exercise bench and take an overgrip on the bar, your hands set three or four inches wider than your shoulders on each side. Straighten your arms to take the barbell off the rack and hold the weight at straight arms' length directly above your

Barbell Bench Press—finish.

shoulder joints. Slowly bend your arms and lower the barbell downward to touch the middle of your chest lightly. Press the weight back to the starting position by straightening your arms. As you lower and raise the weight, be careful that your upper arm bones travel directly out to the sides at right angles with your torso. Allowing your upper arms to travel forward instead of directly outward lessens the stress you place on your pectorals with this movement. Bench Presses can also be done with two dumbbells.

Barbell Incline Press—start, left; finish, right.

Barbell Incline Presses

The *Barbell Incline Press* is similar to a Bench Press, except that exercises done on an incline bench shift stress to the upper pectorals. Lie back on the incline bench, straddling the seat at the bottom end of the bench if there is a seat. Take the same grip on a barbell as for Bench Presses and straighten your arms to lift the barbell from the rack to straight arms' length directly above your shoulder joints. Slowly bend your arms to lower the barbell down to touch your upper chest, being careful to keep your elbows back during the movement. Slowly press the barbell back to the starting point. As with Bench Presses, you can do Incline Presses with two dumbbells.

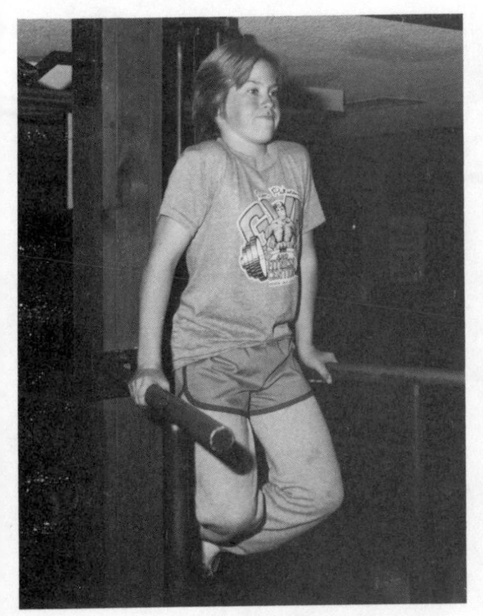

Parallel Bar Dips—start, left; finish, right.

Parallel Bar Dips

The best lower pectoral movement is the *Parallel Bar Dip*. Dips also stress the frontal deltoids and triceps. Take a grip on the parallel bars so your palms are facing each other when you are in the starting position of the movement. Jump up to support your body at straight arms' length, bend your legs at 90-degree angles, and cross your ankles. From this starting position, slowly bend your arms and lower your body as far down between the bars as possible. To put maximum stress on your pecs you should incline your torso forward as you do the movement. Performing Dips with an erect torso transfers major stress to your triceps muscles. When Dips become easy to do you can tie a light dumbbell around your waist.

Flyes

Flyes are a good pectoral isolation movement, particularly for adding shape to the muscles. Grasp two moderately weighted dumbbells and lie back on a flat exercise bench. Extend your arms directly above your chest. Bend them slightly and keep them bent this much throughout the movement. You should also keep your palms facing inward and upward during the movement. From this starting position, lower the dumbbells in semicircles directly out to the sides until they are below the level of your chest. Using pectoral strength, move them back along the same arcs to the starting point. You can also do Flyes on an incline bench if you wish to stress your upper pecs more directly. And you can do Flyes and Bench Presses on a decline bench (an angled bench on which you lie with your head at the lower end) if you desire to stress your lower pectorals more directly.

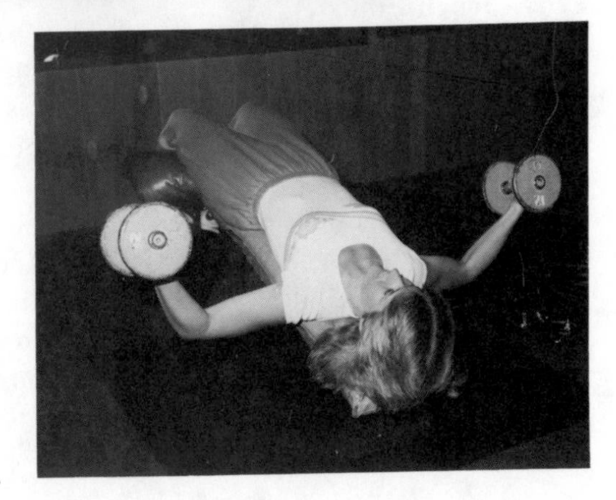

Flyes—start, opposite page; finish, above; on incline, center; and on decline, bottom.

Cross-Bench Pullovers—start.

Cross-Bench Pullovers

A good all-around pectoral and rib cage expansion exercise is *Cross-Bench Pullovers.* This movement is a little tricky to do, so pay extra attention to the exercise photos as you read this description.

Place a moderately weighted dumbbell on its end toward one end of a flat bench. Sit to one side of the bench and place your feet on the floor a little ahead of your hips. Arch your back and raise your hips so your shoulders and upper back are against the top surface of the bench, your face is upward, and your body is perpendicular to the bench. Reach to the side and place your palms against the inside of the upper plates of the dumbbell,

Cross-Bench Pullovers—finish.

being sure that your thumbs encircle the dumbbell handle as it hangs perpendicular to the floor during the movement. Pull the dumbbell into a position directly above your shoulder joints and bend your arms slightly throughout the movement. From this starting position, slowly lower the dumbbell in a semicircular arc downward and backward to as low a position behind your head as possible. Raise the dumbbell back along the same arc to the starting point and repeat the movement. As you become more experienced with Cross-Bench Pullovers you will discover that you can get a better stretch in your chest muscles if you drop your hips a bit as you lower the dumbbell to the bottom point of the movement.

Military Press—start, left; finish, right.

SHOULDER EXERCISES

Military Presses

The *Military Press* is the most basic deltoid exercise. It strongly stresses the frontal deltoids and places secondary stress on the rest of the deltoid muscle group, triceps, upper pectorals, and trapezius muscles. Take an overgrip on a barbell that is lying on the floor, placing your hands three or four inches wider than shoulder width on each side. Pull the barbell up to your shoulders and stand erect, being sure your elbows are directly beneath the bar. From this position, slowly push the weight directly upward past your face to straight arms' length above your head. Be careful as you press the weight that your torso doesn't lean backward to help it up. Lower the barbell slowly to the starting point and repeat the movement.

Press Behind Neck—start, left; finish, right.

Presses Behind Neck

Doing a *Press Behind Neck* stresses the same muscles as a Military Press but eliminates the possibility of leaning your torso backward to cheat up the weight. Take an overgrip on the bar with your hands set two or three inches wider on each side than the grip you used for Military Presses. Pull the weight up to your shoulders and push it over your head to rest across your shoulders and behind your neck. From this position, push it directly upward to straight arms' length above your shoulder joints. Lower it back to the start. Most bodybuilders prefer to do this movement while seated on a flat exercise bench. Performing any exercise while seated isolates the legs from the movement, automatically making it more strict.

25

Dumbbell Press—start, top left; finish, bottom left; and alternating version, above.

Dumbbell Presses

You can also do a *Dumbbell Press,* which stresses the same muscles as Militaries and Presses Behind Neck. Standing erect, grasp two moderately weighted dumbbells and pull them to your shoulders so your palms are facing forward during the movement. Then simply press the dumbbells directly upward to straight arms' length and lower them back to the starting point. As an alternative method of performance, you can keep your palms facing each other as you do the Dumbbell Presses, or you can do them while seated with either palm position. And many bodybuilders like to do Alternate Dumbbell Presses in which one dumbbell is being pressed upward as the other descends.

Side Laterals—start, left; finish, right.

Side Laterals

To isolate stress more on the medial (side) sections of your deltoids, you can do *Side Laterals.* Grasp two light dumbbells in your hands. Stand with your feet set at about shoulder width and rest the dumbbells against each other in front of your hips, your palms facing inward. Lean your torso slightly forward and keep your arms a bit bent throughout the movement. Keeping your palms down, slowly raise the dumbbells in semicircles directly out to the sides until they are slightly above shoulder level. Lower them back to the starting point and repeat the movement.

Bent Laterals—start, left; finish, right.

Bent Laterals

Bent Laterals isolate stress on the posterior (rear) sections of your deltoids. Grasp two light dumbbells, set your feet at about shoulder width, and bend over until your torso is parallel to the floor. Unlock your knees to remove stress from your lower back. Hang the dumbbells directly down from your shoulders, your palms facing each other and your arms slightly bent. Keeping your palms toward the floor, slowly raise the dumbbells in semicircles out to the sides until they are a bit above shoulder level. Lower them back to the starting point.

Barbell Curl—start.

ARM EXERCISES

Barbell Curls

The *Barbell Curl* is the most basic biceps exercise. It also stresses the forearm muscles to a small degree. Take a shoulder-width undergrip (with your palms facing in the opposite direction

Barbell Curl—finish.

from an overgrip) on a barbell and stand erect. Straighten your arms and press your upper arms against the sides of your torso. Keeping your upper arms motionless, use your biceps strength to slowly move the barbell in a semicircle from the tops of your thighs to a point beneath your chin. Slowly lower it back along the same arc to the starting position.

Dumbbell Curl—start, left; finish, right.

Dumbbell Curls

You can do a *Dumbbell Curl* to bomb the same muscles as a Barbell Curl, except that you can stress your biceps even more strongly with Dumbbell Curls. Grasp two moderately weighted dumbbells and allow your arms to hang down at the sides of your body with your palms facing each other. Slowly curl the dumbbells upward, simultaneously rotating your palms 90 degrees so they are facing upward at the top of the movement. This wrist twisting is called *supination,* and it very strongly stresses the biceps muscles. Slowly lower the dumbbells back to the starting point, simultaneously rotating your palms back to the position in which they are facing each other.

Focus on supination of wrist and arm.

Dumbbell Concentration Curl—start, left; finish, right.

Dumbbell Concentration Curls

Bodybuilders perform the *Dumbbell Concentration Curl* to accentuate the natural peak of their biceps. Sit at the end of a flat exercise bench and position your feet about six inches wider on each side than shoulder width. Grasp a light dumbbell in your left hand. Lean forward and pin the back of your left upper arm against the inside of your left leg near your knee. Turn your wrist so your palm is facing directly away from your leg and keep it in this position throughout the movement. Rest your right hand or wrist on your right knee. From this position, slowly curl the dumbbell up to your shoulder. Lower it back to the start and repeat the movement. On all exercises for one arm or leg, be sure that you do an equal number of sets and reps for each limb.

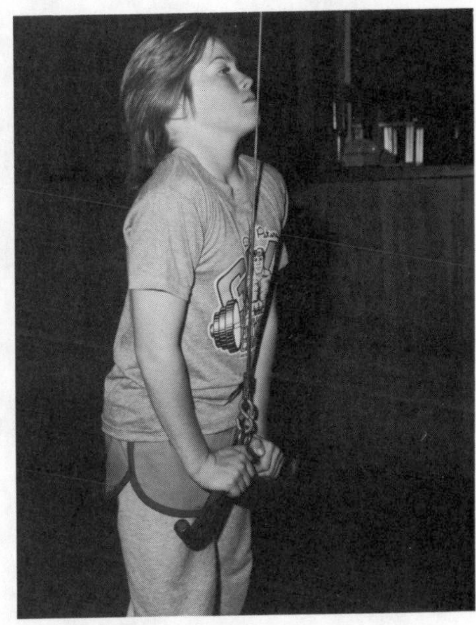

Pulley Pushdown—start, left; finish, right.

Pulley Pushdowns

The *Pulley Pushdown* movement strongly stresses the triceps muscles, particularly the outer heads of the triceps. Stand about a foot back from an overhead pulley and take an overgrip on the angled handle attached to the pulley. Pin your upper arms against the sides of your torso and keep them there throughout the movement. Bend your arms fully. From this starting point, slowly extend your arms, holding the extended position for a moment. Return your arms to the starting point and repeat the movement for the desired number of repetitions.

Lying Barbell Triceps Extension—start, top; finish, bottom.

Lying Barbell Triceps Extensions

You can stress your entire triceps by doing a *Lying Barbell Triceps Extension* movement. Take a narrow overgrip in the middle of a light barbell (there should be about six inches of space between your index fingers). Lie on your back and extend your arms directly above your shoulder joints. Keeping your upper arms motionless, slowly bend your arms and lower the barbell in a semicircular arc downward to touch lightly against your forehead. Use your triceps strength to return the barbell slowly along the same arc to the starting point.

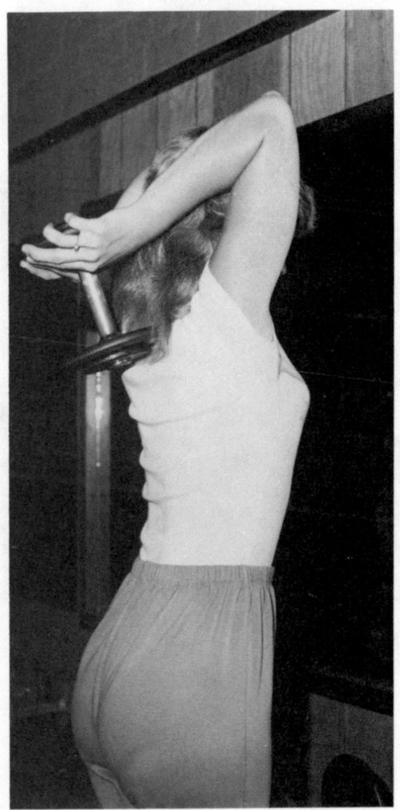

Standing Dumbbell Triceps Extension—start, left; finish, right.

Standing Dumbbell Triceps Extensions

You can also do an excellent *Standing Dumbbell Triceps Extension* movement for the entire triceps muscle complex. Place your palms flat against the inside plates of a dumbbell, the same as you did for your Cross-Bench Pullovers. Standing erect, extend your arms directly upward so the handle of the dumbbell hangs straight downward. Keeping your upper arms against the sides of your head, slowly bend your arms to lower the dumbbell in a semicircular arc to as low a point behind your head as possible. Straighten your arms to return the dumbbell to the starting position.

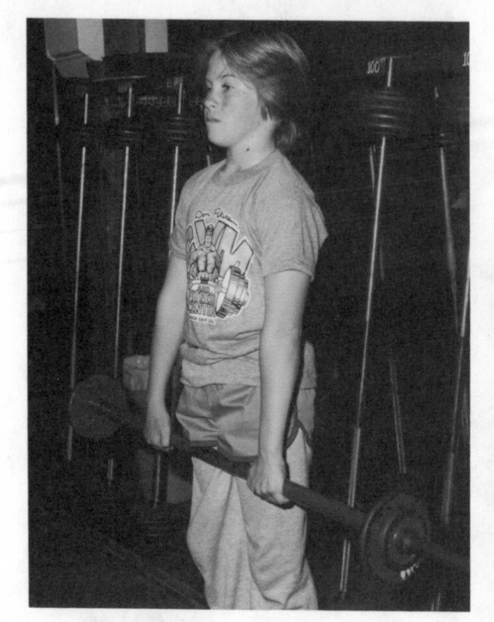

Reverse Curl—start, left; finish, right.

Reverse Curls

The *Reverse Curl* is an excellent barbell movement for stressing the brachialis muscles beneath the biceps and the upper sections of the forearms. Assume the Barbell Curl starting position, except with an overgrip on the bar rather than an undergrip. Bend your arms slowly to curl the weight in an arc from your thighs to a point under your chin. Lower the barbell back to your thighs and repeat.

Barbell Wrist Curl—start, left; finish, right.

Barbell Wrist Curls

A fine direct movement for the powerful flexor muscles on the insides of your forearms is a *Barbell Wrist Curl*. Take a shoulder-width undergrip on a barbell and sit at the end of a flat exercise bench with your feet set at shoulder width. Run your forearms down your thighs so your wrists and fists hang off the edges of your knees. Sag your fists downward as far as you can. From this starting point, slowly curl the barbell upward in a small semicircle by flexing your wrists. Lower the weight back to the starting point and repeat the movement.

Barbell Reverse Wrist Curl—start, above; finish, opposite page.

Barbell Reverse Wrist Curls

If you wish to stress the extensor muscles on the outsides of your forearms, you can do a *Barbell Reverse Wrist Curl.* This movement is executed precisely like a Wrist Curl, except with an overgrip on the barbell. Generally speaking, you will be able to use only about half as much weight for a Reverse Wrist Curl as a Wrist Curl.

Standing Calf Machine Toe Raise—start, left; finish, right. Note toes are pointed out.

CALF EXERCISES

Standing Calf Machine Toe Raises

Toe Raises on a standing calf machine (usually called a *Standing Calf Machine* exercise) are an excellent movement for muscling up the gastrocnemius muscles that make up most of the bulk of your calf. Face the calf machine and dip your knees enough to rest your shoulders under the yokes of the machine. Place your

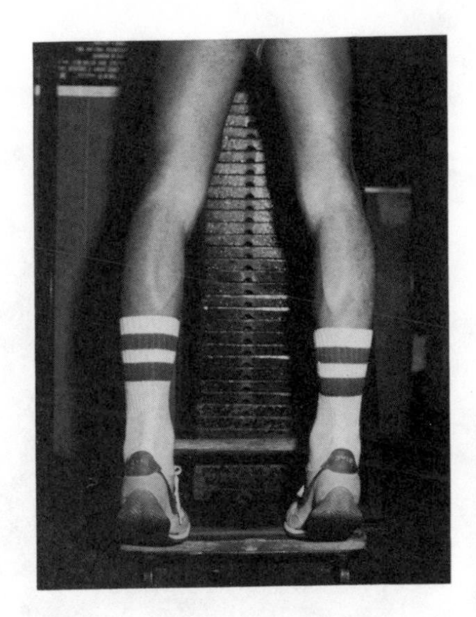

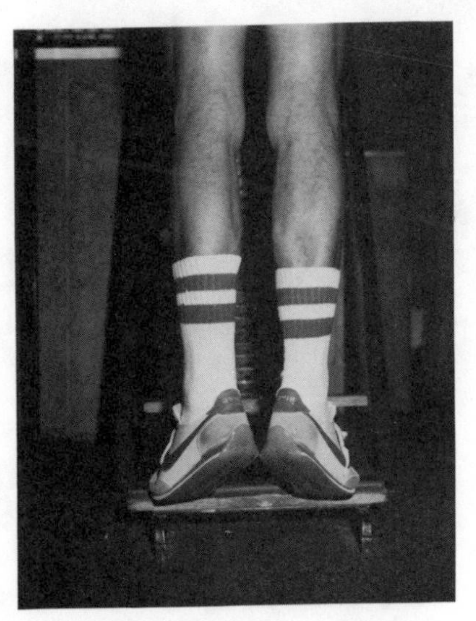

Toe positions—straight ahead, left; in, right.

toes and the balls of your feet on the toe block of the machine. Straighten your legs to take the weight of the machine across your shoulders and keep them straight throughout the movement. Sag your heels as far as you can below the level of your toes to stretch your calf muscles. From this position, slowly rise up as high as you can on your toes. Return to the bottom position and repeat the movement. On all calf exercises you should do some sets with your toes pointed outward at 45-degree angles on each side, some with your toes pointed directly ahead, and some with your toes angled inward at 45 degrees on each side.

Seated Calf Raise Toe Raise—start, left; finish, right.

Seated Calf Machine Toe Raises

Toe Raises on a seated calf machine strongly stress the broad soleus muscles lying under the gastrocnemius muscles, adding greatly to calf width. Sit on the machine's seat and place your toes and the balls of your feet on the toe plate attached to the machine. Pull the padded bar of the machine over the tops of your knees and rise up on your toes enough to move the machine's stop bar forward to release the weight. Sag your heels as far below the level of your toes as possible, then slowly rise up and sag down as far as you can on your toes.

Toe Press—finish.

Toe Presses

If you have a leg press machine available, you can do *Toe Presses* on it. Lie on your back beneath the machine and place your toes and the balls of your feet at the edge of the sliding platform. Straighten your legs and hold them straight throughout the movement. Relax your calves and allow the platform to sag as far below the level of your heels as possible. Then simply extend your feet. Return to the starting point and repeat the movement. There are also leg press machines on which you can sit with your legs parallel to the floor, and they are equally suited for Toe Presses.

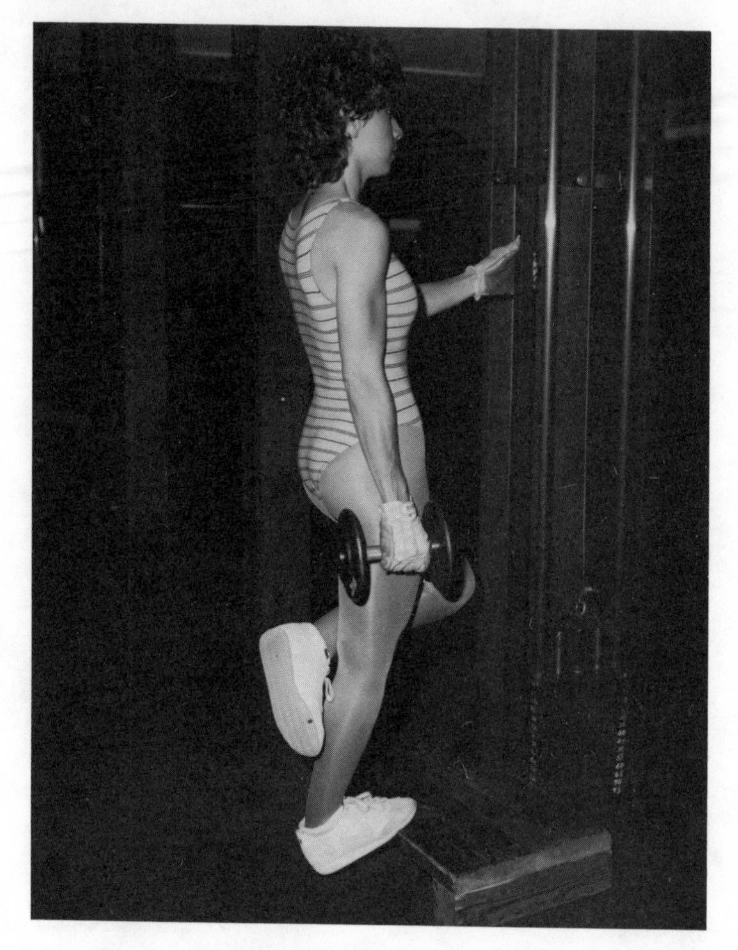

One-Legged Calf Raise—start.

One-Legged Calf Raise

If you train at home and don't have one of the calf machines mentioned above or a leg press machine, you can still do an excellent *One-Legged Calf Raise*. Place the toes and ball of your left foot on a toe block and curl your right foot out of the way.

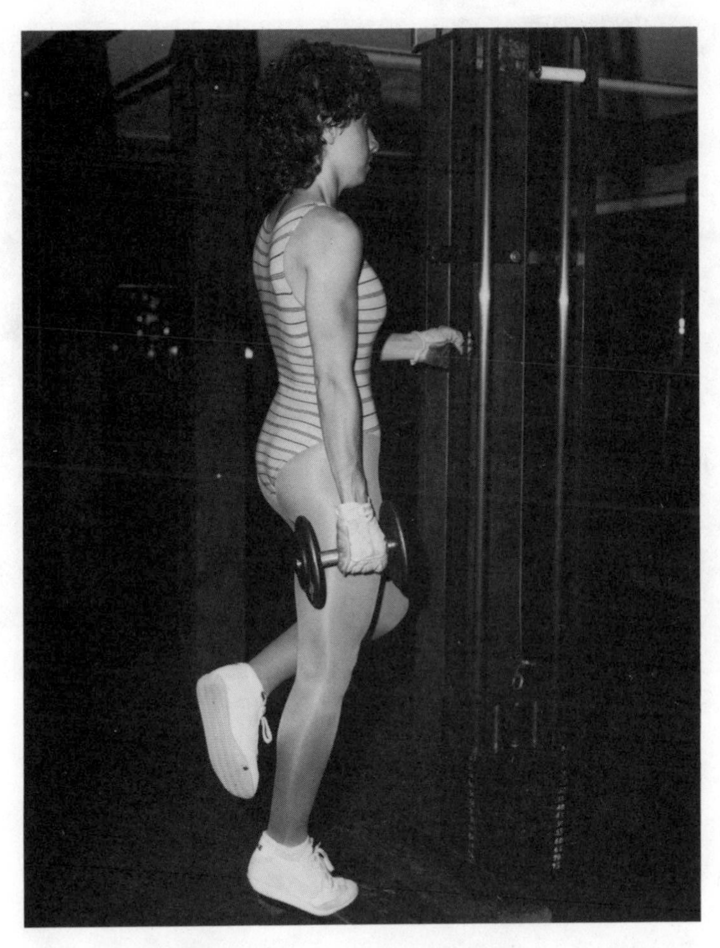

One-Legged Calf Raise—finish.

Hold a dumbbell in your left hand and balance your body during the exercise by holding on to a solid object. Sag your left heel below the level of your toes and then rise up as high as you can on your toes before returning to the stretched position. Be sure to reverse the position described to perform the exercise with your right foot on the block.

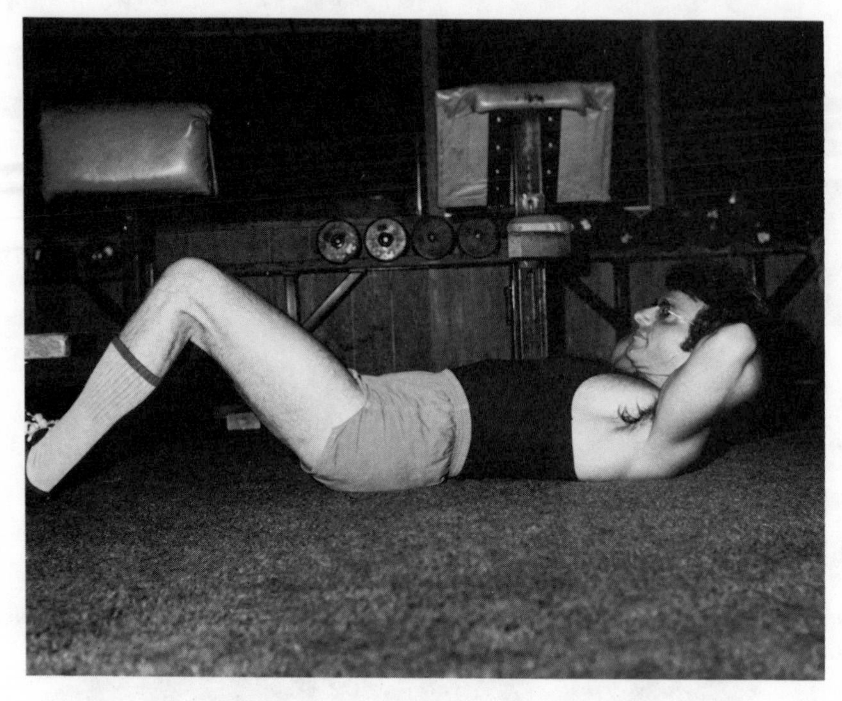

Sit-Up—start.

ABDOMINAL EXERCISES

Sit-Ups

Sit-Ups stress the frontal abdominal muscles, particularly the upper abs. Lie on your back on the floor or on an abdominal board and hook your feet under a heavy piece of furniture or the roller pads of the board. Bend your knees about 30 degrees to remove stress from your lower back as you do the movement. Interlace your fingers behind your head and maintain this arm

Sit-Up—finish.

position throughout the set. From this position, curl your shoulders, then upper back and lower back off the floor or board until your torso is perpendicular to the floor. Never jerk your head and shoulders upward by throwing your arms into the movement, however. Reverse the movement of your torso and return it to the starting position.

Leg Raise—start.

Leg Raises

You can do *Leg Raises* to stress the lower sections of your frontal abdominal muscles. Lie on your back on the floor or on an abdominal board and grasp a heavy piece of furniture or the roller pads of the board. Bend your legs slightly and hold them in this position throughout the movement. From this starting point, slowly raise your feet in semicircles from the floor or board until they are directly above your hips. Slowly lower your feet back to the starting point of the movement.

Leg Raise—finish.

Crunch—start.

Crunches

Crunches are an excellent frontal abdominal isolation movement. Lie on your back on the floor of the gym and rest the backs of your calves over a flat exercise bench, your thighs perpendicular to the floor. Place your hands behind your head as when doing a Sit-Up. From this basic starting position you must simultaneously do four things: (1) use your lower abdominal

Crunch—finish.

strength to raise your hips from the floor; (2) tense your upper abdominals to raise your shoulders from the floor; (3) try to force your shoulders toward your pelvis, thereby shortening your torso; and (4) forcefully blow out all of the air in your lungs. If you do these four things in unison, you will feel a very strong contraction in your frontal abdominal wall. Lower yourself back to the starting point and repeat the movement.

Roman Chair Sit-Up—start, left; finish, right.

Roman Chair Sit-Ups

Roman Chair Sit-Ups are a popular short-range front abdominal exercise that stresses the upper abs. Sit on the seat of a Roman chair and hook your feet under the padded foot bar. Cross your arms over your chest and keep them in this position throughout the movement. Lean your torso backward until it is a bit below a 45-degree angle with the floor. From there, sit forward until you begin to feel tension come off your upper abdominal muscles. Sit back up to the original position. Rock back and forth along this short range of motion for the required number of reps. You can also twist from side to side in this movement to place more stress on your intercostals.

Seated Twisting—start, left; finish, right.

Seated Twisting

You can do *Seated Twisting* to help firm and tone the muscles at the sides of your waist as well as to loosen your lower back before you train. Either sit on a Roman chair and place your feet under the bar or sit on a flat exercise bench and wrap your feet and lower legs around the legs of the bench to hold your body in position throughout the movement. Place a broomstick across your shoulders and entwine your arms around it. From this position, twist vigorously as far as you can to each side, counting one full cycle to each side as a single repetition.

4

Routines

In this chapter I will give you four progressively more intense routines that should hold you for the next four or five months as you progress through the beginning and intermediate phases of training. I have also included a body maintenance routine for those readers who are using this book more to tone and shape their bodies.

It's possible that you won't have the equipment to do an exercise or two that I suggest. If this is the case, simply substitute an equivalent exercise using the equipment you have at hand.

You should change training programs each four to six weeks to keep your mind and body from becoming bored with a particular routine, causing you to stop gaining as quickly as can normally be expected. Many bodybuilders—such as Lou Ferrigno—change their routines more frequently, deciding to move to a new program as soon as they begin to lose interest in the workout they're using. For now, however, you should use each of the following routines for four to six weeks.

First-Level Workout

Monday/Wednesday/Friday

Exercise	Sets	Reps	% Men	% Women
1. Sit-Ups	2–3	20–30	0	0
2. Squats	3	8–12	40	30
3. Barbell Bent Rowing	3	8–12	35	25
4. Bench Presses	3	6–10	30	20
5. Military Presses	2	6–10	25	15
6. Barbell Curls	2	8–12	25	15
7. Lying Triceps Extensions	2	8–12	25	15
8. Standing Calf Machine Toe Raises	3	10–15	30	20
9. Wrist Curls	2	10–15	25	15
10. Reverse Wrist Curls	2	10–15	20	10

Second-Level Workout

Monday/Wednesday/Friday

Exercise	Sets	Reps
1. Leg Raises	2–3	20–30
2. Crunches	2–3	20–30
3. Leg Presses	3	10–15
4. Leg Extensions	2	10–15
5. Leg Curls	3	10–15
6. Hyperextensions	2	10–15
7. Upright Rowing	2	8–12
8. Seated Pulley Rowing	4	8–12
9. Barbell Incline Presses	3	6–10
10. Flyes	2	8–12
11. Side Laterals	2	8–12
12. Bent Laterals	2	8–12
13. Seated Dumbbell Curl	3	8–12

14. Pulley Pushdowns	3	8–12
15. Reverse Curl	2	8–12
16. Wrist Curl	3	10–15
17. Seated Calf Machine	2–3	10–15
18. Calf Press	2–3	15–20

Third-Level Workout

Monday/Thursday

Exercise	Sets	Reps
1. Roman Chair Sit-Ups	2–3	20–30
2. Seated Twisting	2–3	50
3. Squats	4	10–15
4. Leg Extensions	3	10–15
5. Leg Curls	3	10–15
6. Deadlifts	3	6–10
7. Dumbbell Bent Rowing	3	8–12
8. Lat Pulldowns	3	8–12
9. Barbell Shrugs	3	10–15
10. Standing Calf Machine Toe Raises	3	10–15
11. One-Legged Calf Raises	3	10–15
12. Barbell Wrist Curls	3	10–15
13. Barbell Reverse Wrist Curls	3	10–15

Tuesday/Friday

Exercise	Sets	Reps
1. Leg Raises	2–3	20–30
2. Crunches	2–3	20–30
3. Barbell Incline Press	3	6–10
4. Parallel Bar Dips	3	8–12
5. Flyes	2	8–12
6. Seated Press Behind Neck	3	6–10

	Sets	Reps
7. Side Laterals	2	8–12
8. Bent Laterals	2	8–12
9. Pulley Pushdowns	3	8–12
10. Standing Dumbbell Triceps Extensions	2	8–12
11. Barbell Curl	2	8–12
12. Dumbbell Concentration Curl	2	8–12
13. Reverse Curl	2	8–12
14. Barbell Wrist Curl	3	10–15
15. Barbell Reverse Wrist Curl	3	10–15
16. Standing Calf Machine	5	10–15

Fourth-Level Workout

Monday/Thursday

Exercise	Sets	Reps
1. Sit-Ups	2–3	20–30
2. Leg Raises	2–3	20–30
3. Seated Twisting	2–3	50
4. Bench Presses	4	6–10
5. Incline Dumbbell Presses	3	6–10
6. Flat-Bench Flyes	3	8–12
7. Dumbbell Presses	3	6–10
8. Side Laterals	3	8–12
9. Bent Laterals	3	8–12
10. Pulley Pushdowns	3	8–12
11. Lying Triceps Extensions	3	8–12
12. Seated Dumbbell Curls	3	8–12
13. Dumbbell Concentration Curls	3	8–12
14. Barbell Reverse Wrist Curls	4	10–15
15. Seated Calf Machine Toe Raises	4	10–15
16. One-Legged Calf Raises	4	10–15

Tuesday/Friday

Exercise	Sets	Reps
1. Roman Chair Sit-Ups	2–3	20–30
2. Crunches	2–3	20–30
3. Seated Twisting	2–3	50
4. Squats	4	10–15
5. Lunges	3	10–15
6. Leg Curls	4	8–12
7. Hyperextensions	3	10–15
8. Upright Rowing	3	8–12
9. Seated Pulley Rowing	4	8–12
10. Lat Pulldowns	4	8–12
11. Reverse Curls	4	8–12
12. Barbell Wrist Curls	4	10–15
13. Standing Calf Machine Toe Raises	4	10–15
14. Calf Press	4	10–15

Maintenance Workout

Monday/Wednesday/Friday

Exercise	Sets	Reps
1. Roman Chair Sit-Ups	1	30–40
2. Leg Raises	1	20–30
3. Crunches	1	20–30
4. Seated Twisting	1	50
5. Leg Presses	1	10–15
6. Leg Curls	1	10–15
7. Lunges	1	10–15
8. Hyperextensions	1	10–15
9. Upright Rowing	1	8–12
10. Seated Pulley Rowing	1	8–12
11. Lat Pulldowns	1	8–12
12. Incline Barbell Presses	1	8–12

13. Dumbbell Bench Presses	1	8–12
14. Dumbbell Presses	1	8–12
15. Side Laterals	1	8–12
16. Bent Laterals	1	8–12
17. Seated Dumbbell Curls	1	8–12
18. Pulley Pushdowns	1	8–12
19. Dumbbell Concentration Curls	1	8–12
20. Standing Dumbbell Triceps Extensions	1	8–12
21. Reverse Curls	1	8–12
22. Barbell Wrist Curls	1	10–15
23. Barbell Reverse Wrist Curls	1	10–15
24. Standing Calf Machine Toe Raises	1	10–15
25. Seated Calf Machine Toe Raises	1	10–15

Note: Proceed through the maintenance program with no more than 30 seconds of rest between sets.

KEEP PUSHIN'

As you progress through the routines in this chapter your main objective should be to continue adding to your training poundages, but not at the expense of maintaining strict exercise form. Remember that there is a direct relationship between using heavy exercise poundages and having massively developed muscles.

Constantly monitor your physique in the mirror in order to detect weak muscle groups before they lag too far behind the rest of your body. Then you can bomb any lagging muscle group with heavy weights and superintense workouts to bring it up to par with the rest of your physique. In order to become a champion bodybuilder, you *must* keep your body proportions even.

5
Intermediate Techniques

I'm invariably astounded at how many young bodybuilders believe that the champions are keeping secret training techniques from them and that they could also become bodybuilding superstars if they could just learn these secrets. I hereby inform you that *there are no secrets in bodybuilding* past having good heredity and paying your dues in the gym day after day for several years.

Sadly, many young men and women can't see the forest for the trees. Because they are looking so hard for some secret, and easier, way to build quality muscle mass, they fail to notice a number of "open secrets" in the sport. These open secrets are capsulized by a series of single words—dedication, desire, persistence, consistency, intensity, drive, and purpose—that boil down to only two words: *hard work.*

Yes, the true secret to bodybuilding success, if you want to call it a secret, is hard work. There's no easy way to the top. Winston

Churchill had it right when he told the embattled English people during the early days of World War II, "I promise you nothing but blood, sweat, tears, and toil." Every champion bodybuilder has made it to the top by sacrificing the unimportant pleasures of life for thousands of sweaty hours in the gym. And, that's the fact.

I never told you it would be easy, did I?

TRAINING PARTNERS

While the sport has a few introverts who prefer to train alone, most good bodybuilders feel they make better progress when they work out with a training partner. You need a partner to spot you and help with advanced training techniques like forced reps (which will be discussed a little later in this chapter). Over and above this, however, a training partner is a great source of moral support.

A good partner can push you to complete a rep or two past what you could do on your own, and these extra reps are the ones that count. Additionally, it's much more difficult to miss a workout when you know someone is waiting patiently for you down at the gym.

Lou Ferrigno summarized the value of a training partner to a competing bodybuilder: "I simply couldn't get into competitive condition without a training partner. A good workout partner makes me train both harder and faster, and that's guaranteed to get me into contest-winning shape."

Traditionally, men have been training partners for men and women have trained with women. Recently, however, more women have been training with men. Rachel McLish: "I think that training with a man from time to time gives my workouts a boost. Men are much stronger, but they don't have a woman's endurance. These gender differences complement each other quite well. A male partner inspires me to train heavier, while I push him to train harder and longer. This way, we're both winners."

TRAINING TO FAILURE

After six to eight weeks of steady training you should begin to train to failure on one or two sets for each muscle group. You should gradually carry more sets to failure, until every post-warm-up set is pushed as far as you can take it on your own.

Training to failure is a concept fundamental to several workout intensification techniques, such as cheating and forced reps, discussed in the next two sections. It involves continuing a set until you literally cannot complete a full repetition of the exercise. As an example, you might do Barbell Curls in strict form until your biceps are momentarily so fatigued that the barbell stalls out less than halfway up on your final repetition.

A few bodybuilders, such as Tom Platz (Mr. Universe), take training to failure even further than just described. Tom will continue a set doing partial reps (called *burns* by champion bodybuilders) after failing a full rep, until he is unable to move the weight even a couple of inches. Training to total failure like this is grueling, but it pays big dividends in muscle mass. Tom Platz has used training to failure to become one of the most massively muscular bodybuilders of all time.

CHEATING

The most fundamental way to continue a set past the point of normal failure—and hence to stress the muscles even harder than normal to promote faster growth—is to use the cheating method. In Chapter 2, I suggested that you train in very strict form. This is because most novice bodybuilders inadvertently cheat in an exercise to make it *easier* to do rather than harder. As an intermediate, however, I feel you are experienced enough to use the cheating principle to make a set even *harder* on your working muscles.

One of the first exercises that a bodybuilder incorrectly cheats on is Barbell Curls, so let's use it in an example of how to cheat correctly. Choose a weight with which you can do six to eight strict reps before failing; then do those repetitions to momentary muscular failure. Only at this point should you swing your torso back and forth *just enough* to propel the barbell past the "sticking point" at which the weight stalled out on the final rep. The rest of the curl must be done with biceps strength alone.

Once you have curled the weight up to your neck, lower it slowly back to the starting position, resisting its downward momentum as strongly as possible with your fatigued biceps. It is very important that you use only enough body swing to get the weight up and then strongly resist it as you lower the bar. Generally, two or three cheating repetitions will be sufficient to push your biceps to the point at which additional cheating reps would be unproductive.

Many bodybuilders begin a set in strict form, then loosen up a bit with each succeeding rep as their biceps become more fatigued. As long as you do at least four or five strict reps before beginning to cheat, this is one of the best ways to use the cheating method.

You can use cheating on most free-weight exercises, and it's a valuable training method as long as you are careful to begin a set with strict reps. Always keep in mind that you must use cheating to make a set harder, not easier, to do.

FORCED REPS

If you have a training partner, you can use forced reps instead of cheating to push a set past the point of failure. In this method your partner progressively pulls upward a little harder on the weight for each repetition past the failure point as your working muscles become more fatigued.

Let's use the Bench Press to illustrate how to use forced reps to saturation bomb your pecs, delts, and triceps. If you're using 200 pounds (100 pounds for women) and fail with the sixth repetition of a set, this only means that you are too fatigued to do a rep with 200 (100) pounds. Without a doubt, you can still do a rep with 190 (95), a second with 180 (90), and perhaps a third with 170 (85) pounds.

So, your training partner's task is to stand at the head end of the bench and pull up on the center of the bar *only enough* for you to force out two or three extra reps. As with cheating reps, more than two or three forced reps will be unnecessary, since that number of repetitions will almost completely exhaust your pectorals, deltoids, and triceps.

You can do forced reps on numerous exercises, but it's easiest to use this training technique on barbell exercises and movements done on machines. It's a bit clumsy to do forced reps with dumbbells and cables, though it can be done.

It's possible to give yourself forced reps on one-armed exercises. I've often seen Mike Mentzer (Mr. America, Mr. Universe) give himself a couple of forced reps on Dumbbell Concentration Curls by pushing against the wrist of his working hand with the fingers of his free hand. The same can be done on a number of other one-armed movements.

In my observation most bodybuilders use forced reps in their training, though a few have found that extensive use of forced reps is a bit too draining. If you discover this to be true in your own case, simply back off on the number of sets you push past failure.

SUPERSETS

Supersets are another good method for intensifying your training. They are groupings of two exercises done with minimum rest between sets, followed by a normal rest interval of approximately 60 seconds and other supersets. Since you can do more total sets in a fixed time using supersets, they are more intense than straight sets.

The most basic form of superset is formed of exercises for antagonistic muscle groups such as the biceps and triceps, pectorals and lats, or quadriceps and hamstrings. Here are examples of such supersets:

Biceps + Triceps = Dumbbell Curls + Pulley Pushdowns
Pecs + Lats = Bench Presses + Lat Pulldowns
Quads + Hamstrings = Leg Extensions + Leg Curls

This is the first type of superset you should try in your workouts. Begin with a biceps and triceps superset, then work additional supersets into your training sessions. You may discover—as Lou Ferrigno did—that supersets don't allow you to add muscle mass to your body, however. Lou discovered that he must stick to forced reps in his own training, because supersets cause his muscles to lose mass.

A second, and much more intense, type of superset involves doing two movements for a single muscle group. After the discussion of basic and isolation exercises in the next section I will tell you how to use this type of superset in the preexhaustion training method.

BASIC VERSUS ISOLATION EXERCISES

Basic exercises are those that work large muscle groups such as the thighs and pectorals in conjunction with smaller groups like the biceps and triceps. In contrast, isolation exercises are those that stress only a single muscle group (or even a part of a muscle) in relative isolation from the rest of the body.

In the table below I have listed common basic and isolation exercises for each major muscle group.

Basic and Isolation Exercises

Muscle	Basic Exercises	Isolation Exercises
Thighs	Squats, Leg Presses, Deadlifts	Leg Extensions, Leg Curls
Lats	Seated Pulley Rowing, Bent Rowing, Lat Pulldowns	Pullovers
Trapezius	Upright Rows	Shrugs
Pectorals	Bench Presses, Incline Presses, Parallel Bar Dips	Incline/Decline/Flat Flyes
Biceps	Barbell Curls	Dumbbell/Barbell Concentration Curls
Triceps	Lying Triceps Extensions	Pulley Pushdowns

In general, basic movements are best for stressing the large muscle groups of the body with heavy weights to build muscle mass. Isolation exercises are better for shaping and ripping up a muscle prior to competition. Top bodybuilders use more basic movements in an off-season mass- and power-building cycle and a larger percentage of isolation exercises during a precontest training phase.

PREEXHAUSTION

Basic exercises for the torso muscles often do not allow you to blast your pecs, lats, and delts to the limit, because the smaller biceps and triceps muscles grow fatigued and fail to move a barbell long before the torso muscles have been fully blasted. To circumvent this problem, bodybuilders use the preexhaustion technique.

In preexhaustion you will superset an isolation exercise to weaken the torso muscle group with a basic movement to push the muscles as far as possible into the fatigue zone while the arm muscles are momentarily stronger. This might seem overly complicated to you, so let's train your pectorals with a preexhaustion superset of Flyes and Bench Presses to illustrate the technique.

Begin with a full set of six to eight reps of Flyes to the point of failure, being sure to lie on a pressing bench with a loaded barbell on the rack. Place the dumbbells on the floor and *immediately* do a set of Bench Presses to failure. It's essential that you rest minimally between the two exercises, because any rest interval longer than 5–10 seconds will allow your pectorals to recuperate sufficiently to destroy the preexhaustion effect.

If you immediately perform the Benches, however, your pectorals will be so fatigued that they will be relatively much weaker than your triceps, even though they are normally several times as strong and enduring as your arm muscles. As a result, your triceps will briefly be strong enough for you to stress your pecs far more with the Bench Presses than if you hadn't first preexhausted them with Flyes.

Following are several preexhaustion supersets that you can gradually phase into your workouts:

Upper Pecs = Incline Flyes + Incline Presses

Lower Pecs = Decline Flyes + Decline Presses

Pecs (in general) = Flat-Bench Flyes + Bench Presses

Deltoids = Side Laterals + Presses Behind Neck

Deltoids = Upright Rowing + Military Presses

Lats = Pullovers + Lat Pulldowns

Traps = Shrugs + Upright Rows

When you do heavy Squats your lower back can often be a weak point that prevents your thighs from being blitzed as totally as they should be. In such a case you can superset Leg Extensions (to preexhaust your thighs) with Squats. Casey Viator (history's youngest Mr. America winner at age 19) took this preexhaustion technique for thighs to the limit, doing these three exercises for 15–20 reps each set with ponderous poundages—Leg Presses (with 750 pounds), Leg Extensions (more than 300), and Squats (more than 500). Even with only one set of each movement, *that* is using preexhaustion to train the thighs with maximum intensity!

OVERTRAINING

If you get too enthusiastic about your training and do excessive sets in each workout, it is likely that you will overtrain. This is a condition in which you are too exhausted to cope with additional workouts and still make muscle gains. The most common symptoms of overtraining are chronic fatigue, sore joints and muscles, an unwillingness to go to the gym, lack of appetite, and insomnia.

Overtraining has much in common with being overdrawn at the bank. If you regularly make deposits equal to or greater than the amount for which you write checks, the bank won't hassle you. But if you write checks for more than you deposit, you soon overdraw your account and the bank is likely to close it.

Similarly, your body is a dynamic energy exchange system in which you pay out energy in each workout and deposit it by sleeping and resting, eating the right foods, and maintaining a tranquil mind. If you expend more energy than you deposit for a long enough period of time, you will go energy "broke," or overtrain.

Without fail, bodybuilders overtrain when they work out too much, not when they train too hard. Therefore, you can avoid overtraining by doing shorter and more intense workouts rather than the long, marathonlike routines you see written up in bodybuilding magazines. These magazine workouts are usually precontest regimens followed for only a few weeks prior to a major competition. For the rest of the year champion bodybuilders do shorter and harder workouts, so don't be fooled into overtraining by what you read in the mags.

If you become overtrained, you should first take a one-week layoff from the weights. Then, when you start going back to the gym, switch to a totally new routine. If you're careful to perform short, high-intensity workouts once you're back into training, you'll be able to avoid overtraining in the future.

Taking an occasional one-week layoff from training can often be an effective deterrent to overtraining. One week off every four to six months will do the trick, but be sure that you don't take a layoff merely to avoid the gym. Some "bodybuilders" seem to spend more time on layoffs than actually training.

TRAINING INJURIES

It's possible that you will work out for a lifetime without incurring a training injury. Avoiding injuries is primarily a matter of warming up completely, maintaining a fast enough workout pace to keep from cooling off, using proper biomechanical positions in all exercises, and using sound judgment in choosing maximum training poundages. Still, an unforeseen accident can result in an injury, so you must understand how to handle routine training injuries.

If an injury is disabling, you should immediately consult your family physician and follow his recommendations. Included in this category are dislocated joints, broken bones, and severe strains and sprains. I haven't, incidentally, seen an injury this severe occur in a gym, and I've spent literally thousands of hours in bodybuilding gyms in my 23 years of involvement in the sport.

The most common bodybuilding training injuries are muscle strains and minor joint sprains. Typically, the symptom of these injuries is a mildly sore muscle or painful lower back. Such an injury is usually sensed as a sharper pain during a workout, with a milder—although uncomfortable—pain for several days afterward. You're most likely to suffer this type of injury when you lift a heavy weight using awkward form, particularly when you have allowed your body to cool a bit by talking with someone between sets.

If there is no pain in the muscle or joint a day after an injury, you needn't worry about it except for merely going a little lighter (say 20–25 percent less than your normal workout poundages) on any movements that stress the injured area. More serious injuries should initially be iced to prevent swelling, then rested for several days until pain has abated. Just rub the area for five minutes every hour or two with an ice cube.

Beginning 36–48 hours after the injury, you should start applying heat to the area, preferably with a hot water bottle wrapped in a damp towel. Damp heat like this is conducted into the injury site more readily than dry heat.

Once you are sure that pain has abated, resume light weight work for the tender area, gradually increasing the weight used each workout until you're back to normal. Back off on the poundage if you feel any minor pain in the injured area, however, and work up again a bit more slowly.

By following the foregoing injury treatment procedure, you will no doubt be back to normal training within two or three weeks after an injury. But, by maintaining proper biomechanics in all exercises and keeping warm during your workouts, you will avoid training injuries.

EXERCISE MACHINES

There is a wide variety of exercise machines—mainly manufactured by Nautilus Sports-Medical Industries and Universal Gyms—that I have not discussed in Chapter 3. I have nothing against these exercise machines, because they are excellent apparatus for bodybuilding training. They certainly aren't the be-all, end-all for bodybuilding that many claim, but in conjunction with free weights and related apparatus, they will help you make good muscle gains.

I feel that the vast majority of readers will have little access to this equipment, however, so in this book I have presented a good basic training course using free weights. And you will easily be able to add exercises using machines to your workouts as you learn these new movements.

I would be remiss, however, if I didn't inform you of the advantages and disadvantages of using exercise machines. Beginning with the first advantage, machines provide totally safe training, since they are constructed to remove any chance of a weighted bar dropping across the body.

The type of resistance provided by exercise machines—particularly Nautilus—is superior to that given by most free-weight exercises. They provide resistance directly against a muscle throughout its full range of motion, and in many of the machines the resistance provided is balanced with the normal strength curve of a muscle (i.e., the machine provides greater resistance at points along the range of motion of an exercise where the muscles are naturally stronger).

There are two main disadvantages to using exercise machines. First, there are so few exercises that can be done for a specific body part with each brand of machine that a serious bodybuilder will quickly become bored with training on the machines. Second, machines are extremely expensive, certainly far more costly than a novice bodybuilder can afford in equipping his or her home gym.

Go ahead and try the exercise machines you encounter. Just be sure to treat them as a *supplement* to free-weight exercises.

INDIVIDUALIZED ROUTINES

By the time you have completed using the routines suggested in Chapter 4—possibly even sooner—you should begin making up your own training programs. To do so, you should draw from the exercises presented in this book, plus any other movements you see done in a gym or discover in reading other bodybuilding books and magazines.

I could continue suggesting workouts for years, but it's far better for you to assume this responsibility as soon as it is feasible, because only *you* can sense how new exercises and techniques affect your body. I can't project myself into your body to feel how your exercises and routines are working for you.

Begin your task by using the Third-Level and Fourth-Level routines in Chapter 4 as guidelines to how your routines should look. Then follow these rules for formulating future personalized training programs:

1. Continue to learn as much as you can by reading all of the bodybuilding books and magazines you can lay your hands on (see Chapter 7) and by discussing bodybuilding training with champion bodybuilders available to you.
2. Always do your torso movements prior to your arm exercises, so you don't make your arms any weaker than they already are in relation to your torso muscles (see the discussion of preexhaustion earlier in this chapter).
3. You can do your abdominal and/or calf workout at the beginning of your training session as a further full-body warm-up. Always perform your forearm program near the end of your workout, because it will impede your ability to grip the weights in other exercises.
4. Position the exercises for any lagging muscle group early in your workout (see the discussion of muscle priority training later in this chapter).
5. For the next few months—perhaps for as long as the next year or two—continue following a four-day split routine in which each major muscle group is worked twice per week. You can train your abdominals and calves in each session on a four-day split.

6. Be sure that you don't do too many sets for each muscle group, or you will overtrain. For larger body parts (thighs, back, chest), you should do no more than 10–12 total sets, unless you have progressed to the stage at which you are placing in the competitions you enter. Smaller muscle groups (deltoids, biceps, triceps, forearms) will respond best to a total of no more than six to eight sets per body part. Calves should be stressed with six to eight total sets as well, perhaps doing 8–10 twice per week and only four to six the other two workouts. I would suggest doing between five and 10 sets for your abdominals, five or six if they are well toned and up to 10 if they need additional work.

7. Always perform at least one basic exercise for each muscle group and fill in the rest of each training schedule for a body part with isolation exercises and perhaps another basic movement.

8. Train your larger muscle groups first in your workout whenever possible, because when you're running out of gas toward the end of a training session it's much easier to continue working a smaller muscle like your biceps with good intensity than a larger one such as your thighs. Here is a ranking of the various muscle groups from largest to smallest—thighs, back, chest, calves, deltoids, triceps, biceps, forearms, and abdominals.

MUSCLE PRIORITY TRAINING

In Rule 4 of the foregoing section I suggested that you place the workout for a lagging body part near the beginning of a training session. You must do this, because you can only blast a lagging muscle group with maximum energy early in a workout, when your physical and mental energies are at a peak.

This practice of training weak body parts first is called *muscle priority training,* and it is the essence of a bodybuilder's search for perfect proportions. As I told you in Chapter 1, one of the main goals that a competitive bodybuilder should maintain is a perfect proportional balance among all of the body's muscle groups, and muscle priority training is the best tool you have at your command for accomplishing this goal.

Constantly observe your developing physique in a mirror and in photos to detect weaknesses before they fall too far behind your physique to be brought back up. And, when you discover a lagging muscle group, you should immediately move it toward the beginning of your workout, where you can blast it with greatly augmented physical and mental intensity. Don't get carried away with doing added sets, however. Instead, use preexhaustion, heavier weights, and forced reps on your exercises for the weak muscle group.

If you consistently saturation bomb a lagging body part like this and stress it early in your workout when you have all of your energy reserves intact, it will grow relatively quickly and will soon be up to par with the rest of your physique.

BODYBUILDING DRUGS

If you haven't already heard about bodybuilding drugs—most of which are called *steroids*—you will shortly become aware of them. Many champion male bodybuilders—and even a few women—use anabolic steroids to add to their muscle mass. And many young bodybuilders are tempted to use these muscle growth drugs as well.

Unless you are a national-level bodybuilder, however, I personally feel that it is foolish—even dangerous—to use anabolics. Even at a high competitive level, the choice to use or not use steroids is a personal one that you should make only after consulting a physician who has had experience in administering anabolic steroids to male athletes. Women—in the opinion of Rachel McLish, Laura Combes, and every other woman bodybuilder with whom I've talked—should stay clear of any steroid usage.

At the beginning and intermediate levels of bodybuilding involvement, steroid use is dangerous. A young bodybuilder who takes steroids will gain muscle mass fairly quickly, but soon the steroids in his system will cause his normal level of testosterone secretion to diminish.

As your testosterone production gradually shuts down, the steroids will have less and less effect, which tempts many naive bodybuilders to use larger and larger doses of the drugs. And, if a young bodybuilder later goes off steroids, his own testosterone production will have become so low that his body will invariably be unable to support the larger degree of muscle mass that the drugs helped to add. As a result, the young bodybuilder almost immediately loses all of the precious muscle tissue he worked so hard to build up.

From that point a vicious cycle often develops. The young bodybuilder goes right back on steroids to keep the muscle mass, and he is forced to stay on the drugs for long periods of time, which greatly magnifies the risk of dangerous side effects from steroid usage.

So, stay away from bodybuilding drugs as long as you can. If you take them, do so only when you have reached a high level of development and have carefully investigated and weighed the possible health hazards that inevitably come with their use.

6

Basic Bodybuilding Nutrition

Most champion bodybuilders feel that following a proper diet is 50 percent of the battle in building a great physique. I agree. Prior to a competition a good dietary approach may be as much as 75–80 percent responsible for a champion bodybuilder's on-stage condition.

I'm sure that there is as much to learn about bodybuilding nutrition as there is to learn about bodybuilding training, so I urge you to read every nutrition article you come across in the various bodybuilding magazines. This will help you begin acquiring a more sophisticated knowledge of the subject.

There are also many nutrition books available at most health food stores, and you should begin to read them as well. Be careful, however, that you sort the fact from the myth that a lot of these books contain. There is considerable faddist literature in the nutrition field, so you should be careful to correlate data read in several sources before you fully accept them.

To give you a starting point before you do your magazine and book readings, here are lists of basic "dos" and "don'ts" in bodybuilding nutrition.

DON'T

1. Don't consume junk foods (those that are made with sugar and/or white flour are highly processed, or are fried).
2. Don't consume excessive animal fats. Eat more low-fat meats (poultry and fish) and be sure to trim all excess fat from beef and pork before eating these high-fat meats. Consume fewer full-fat milk and other dairy products.
3. Don't use extra salt on your foods. Avoid food that is highly seasoned. Avoid diet sodas, which have a high sodium content.
4. Don't consume excessive amounts of alcohol; avoid sugared soft drinks.

DO

1. Eat a small amount of protein at each meal. The best sources of protein are poultry, fish, eggs, and nonfat milk products. Secondary protein sources include beef, pork, full-fat milk products, lentils, rice, corn, seeds, and nuts. You should consume only small amounts of protein at each meal, because your body can digest and use only 20–30 grams of protein at each meal. Therefore, huge protein meals are largely wasted.
2. Eat a wide variety of fresh fruits, vegetables, and salads. Whenever possible, eat your vegetables raw rather than cooked. And, when you do eat cooked vegetables, try to have them steamed rather than boiled to retain nutrients.
3. Consume a little vegetable fat each day from grains, seeds, and nuts. Contrary to what many bodybuilders believe, you need some fat in your diet to keep your body—and particularly your nerves—in good health.
4. Eat at least three meals per day, aiming to consume up to six relatively small meals each day. Your body can digest and utilize smaller snacks much more easily and efficiently than large meals.

5. Drink plenty of pure water, particularly distilled water. Water is one of the best body-cleansing agents that nature has provided.

6. Include in your diet at least one multiple vitamin-mineral capsule per day. It would be even better to take one or two multipacks of vitamins and minerals each day with your meals. Vitamins and minerals are best utilized by your body when consumed with other foods.

7. In general, eat with as much variety as possible. Each food has a unique spectrum of vitamins, minerals, and other nutrients. It has more of one and less of another than all other foods. So, you stand the best chance of eating a balanced diet when you consume the widest possible variety of fresh foods.

WEIGHT-GAIN DIET

Champion bodybuilders have concluded that the keys to gaining muscular body weight are heavy training and a high-protein diet. Merely eating larger amounts of protein isn't the answer nutritionally, however. The key is to eat in such a manner that your body can efficiently digest (and make ready for assimilation into muscle tissue) a greater amount of protein *each day*.

As I mentioned in the previous section of this chapter, your body can digest only 20–30 grams of protein at each meal under normal circumstances. Men have larger stomachs than women, and they can efficiently digest a few more grams of protein, hence the range mentioned for protein digestion.

Eating a large meal with 100–150 grams of protein content can actually *reduce* the amount of protein digested at that feeding, because large meals make your digestive system less efficient. You will actually digest more total protein in a meal containing 30 grams of the food element than you would in a meal with 130 grams, and this fact is central to the plan I will outline for digesting a maximum amount of protein each day.

If your stomach can digest only 20–30 grams of protein at each feeding, you will digest 60–90 grams a day if you eat a normal three meals per day. But, if you eat six times—with two or three hours between meals—you would *double* the amount of protein your stomach digests every day.

So, in the weight-gaining diet followed by most experienced bodybuilders, you should eat five or six smaller meals throughout the day. You more or less snack all day, making sure your snacks are made up of nutritional foods, not junk foods. Many bodybuilders eat solid food at their three normal mealtimes and protein drinks (see the last section of this chapter for a discussion of protein drinks) between meals, an excellent plan as long as you keep your solid-food meals relatively small.

Here is a sample menu for one day of eating five meals per day in order to gain muscular body weight, (assuming a 10:00 p.m. bedtime):

Meal 1 (8:00 a.m.): cheese omelet, glass of milk, supplements.
Meal 2 (11:00 a.m.): protein drink.
Meal 3 (2:00 p.m.): broiled chicken, rice, milk, supplements.
Meal 4 (5:00 p.m.): protein drink.
Meal 5 (8:00 p.m.): broiled fish, baked potato, vegetable, milk, supplements.

Milk is a popular weight-gaining food, and raw (unpasteurized) milk is more usable in the human digestive system. Many individuals can't digest milk, however, because their stomachs produce too little of the digestive enzyme that breaks down the sugar in milk. This problem is more common in men than in women, more frequently observed among Blacks and Orientals than among Caucasians, and increases in frequency as an individual grows older.

If you have this problem, which is called *galactose intolerance,* your stomach will feel bloated with gas soon after drinking milk. You might also feel drowsy and lethargic. You can still eat hard cheeses, however, because the lactose (milk sugar) is removed from milk when cheese is processed.

Many bodybuilders consume digestive enzyme tablets as a means of digesting more protein at each meal. There are many different types of digestive enzymes available at health food stores. These enzyme preparations do help you digest a little more protein, so they are worth trying if your budget can stand the strain. The most commonly available digestive enzymes are papain and bromelain.

You might also find that increased consumption of B-complex vitamins aids in gaining muscular body weight, since the various B vitamins increase tissue synthesis and improve the appetite. You won't need to worry about taking in too much B-complex, however, because B vitamins are water soluble and excesses are eliminated in the urine. It is *conceivable* that you could take in toxic levels of some B vitamins, but, practically speaking, it is impossible to do.

WEIGHT LOSS

When most people think about dieting, they immediately turn their thoughts to losing weight. But, as we have already seen, the general topic of diet is a much more complex issue in bodybuilding.

Through proper diet and weight training (plus 30 minutes of aerobic exercise each day, if possible), you can very easily lose body fat and normalize your weight. It is simply a matter of creating a caloric deficit, or of using up a few more calories each day than you consume in your diet.

For each accumulated deficit of 3,500 calories you will lose one pound of body fat. So, to lose one pound of fat per week, you need only create a deficit of 500 calories each day; for a two-pound weekly loss, you must create a daily caloric deficit of 1,000 calories, which is relatively easy to do when you're working out regularly.

The weight workout you do each day will allow you to expend 250–300 calories each hour, over and above what your body burns up in normal metabolic processes. Another half hour of aerobics will allow you to expend 150–200 calories, so an hour of bodybuilding and a half hour of aerobics each day can give you up to 500 calories to add to your caloric deficit, which in itself would cause you to lose a pound of body fat every week.

It's easier, however, to create a larger caloric deficit by dieting once you are up to an hour of weight work each day. And the easiest way to trim calories out of your diet—above and beyond the obvious step of curtailing your junk food intake—is to reduce your consumption of fats.

One gram of fat yields nine calories when metabolized in your body for energy, while a gram of protein or carbohydrate yields only four grams. So, if fats are more than twice as concentrated a source of calories as protein and carbohydrates, it seems logical that reducing fat intake and replacing the fats with protein and carbs will reduce total caloric consumption. Indeed, this does work, and it's the body fat reduction method used by a majority of champion bodybuilders.

The most obvious sources of fats in most diets are beef, pork, full-fat milk products, oils, and nuts. Less obvious sources of fats include egg yolks, corn, grains, and seeds. So, substituting fish or chicken (without the fatty skin) for red meats in your diet will markedly cut your caloric intake. Fish, incidentally, is lower in calories than poultry.

Here is a sample daily menu for pain-free weight loss through low-fat dieting:

Breakfast: high-bran whole-grain cereal with nonfat milk, fruit, coffee or tea (use fructose as a sweetener), supplements.

Lunch: broiled fish, rice, salad (with vinegar as a dressing), iced tea with fructose.

Dinner: broiled poultry, baked potato (no butter or sour cream), salad, coffee, supplements.

Snacks: raw vegetables, fruit, cold chicken or turkey.

Fructose is an excellent sweetener. It's so sweet for its caloric content that you use far less of it than sugar for the same sweetening effect. Artificial sweeteners are self-defeating, because they contain sodium, which will bloat your body with water.

Be very careful when dieting to strictly limit the number of calories you drink each day. You can drink 1,000 calories of orange juice in two or three minutes, but it would take a half hour or more to eat 1,000 calories worth of oranges. Why not enjoy eating the fruit, especially when you'd consume less than

1,000 calories if you ate the whole fruit, instead of drinking the juice?

You will feel a little low in energy when on a diet. You actually must feel this way in order to lose body fat. But if you really feel wasted, eat a piece or two of fruit. Forcing yourself to eat so little food that you go into a large energy debt is an open invitation to binge eating. In the long run you'll be far better off if you lose body fat slowly and easily.

FOOD SUPPLEMENTS

Champion bodybuilders are very fastidious in their use of food supplements—concentrated proteins, vitamins, and minerals. I've often seen one of them swallow 20–30 capsules and tablets at a meal.

As you grow more experienced, you too will experiment with a wide spectrum of vitamins and minerals. For now, however, it's best to take one or two of the vitamin and mineral multipacks mentioned earlier in this chapter. If you wish to take extra vitamins and minerals, the best to experiment with initially are vitamin C, the B-complex vitamins, potassium, and calcium.

At this point the area in which you can best use food supplements is in adding protein to your diet with the protein drinks mentioned in the last section. There are many types and brands of protein powders available, and the best ones are made from milk and eggs. Along with fish, milk and eggs contain the proteins of highest biological quality. So, be sure to read the labels on all available brands of protein powder before buying one.

Be sure to use the protein—as well as supplemental vitamins and minerals—as a *supplement* to your diet, not as a substitute for food. Elite bodybuilders do use food supplements but only in moderation. However, I've seen a few misguided novice bodybuilders almost living off food supplements, a very expensive and unnecessary practice.

You'll get much more nutritional value from your protein drinks if you take them between meals rather than with meals.

Indeed, protein drinks are particularly valuable as a quick and convenient replacement for a meal that you might ordinarily have missed.

Here is a good protein drink recipe that you can whip up in a blender:

10 ounces of nonfat raw milk
2 tablespoons of protein powder
fruit to taste

Soft fruits (such as bananas, peaches, and strawberries) are best for use in blender drinks. One piece—or four or five berries—is usually plenty.

7

Sources: Equipment and References

In this concluding chapter I'll tell you where to purchase bodybuilding equipment as well as what pieces of equipment you should initially purchase if you intend to train at home. I'll also recommend a number of books and magazines you should read in order to increase and constantly update your knowledge of bodybuilding.

Equipping Your Home Gym

If you live in a town or city with a commercial gym in it, you should train there because of its wider variety of equipment and the camaraderie available at such an establishment. Even if you decide to train in a home gym, it's best to seek training partners to pool equipment with you and help form a well-equipped cooperative gym.

The first pieces of equipment that you should buy are an adjustable 200-pound barbell and dumbbell set with metal plates (cost: about $120 new) and an adjustable exercise bench ($50–$100 new, depending on which features are included). You can make good progress for two or three months with only this small home-gym equipment outlay, and for an even longer period of time if you are a woman.

As soon as you begin to outgrow your basic barbell set, simply purchase more plates to make it heavier. You can buy these plates new or often used with good discounts at garage and yard sales. With luck and some digging, you can probably buy other used weight equipment that will be of use in a home gym. Or, if you either have carpentry/welding skills or know someone who does, you can build many needed pieces of equipment.

Here are many other pieces of equipment that I've seen in good home gyms: squat racks, EZ-curl bars, leg extension–leg curl machines, hack machines, Roman chairs, abdominal boards, lat pulleys, T-bars, rowing pulleys, dipping and chinning bars, standing and seated calf machines, curling benches, incline benches, decline benches, moon benches, weight racks, mirrors, and rubber weight mats. You won't need all of these pieces of equipment in a home gym, but each helps to make home-gym workouts more productive.

Following are the addresses of several companies that will send you catalogs and brochures of equipment suitable for home use:

Weider Health & Fitness
21100 Erwin St.
Woodland Hills, CA 91367

Marcy
1736 Standard Ave.
Glendale, CA 91201

Robert Kennedy
270 Rutherford Rd. S.
Brampton, Ontario L6W 3K7
Canada

Body Culture Equipment Co.
P. O. Box 10
Alliance, NE 69301

Billiard Barbell Co.
208 Chestnut St.
Reading, PA 19602

Ed Jubinville
Box 662
Holyoke, MA 01040

Tennessee Gym Equipment Co.
Box 5847
Knoxville, TN 37418

Bell Foundry
Box 1070
Southgate, CA 90806

Paramount
3000 S. Santa Fe Ave.
Los Angeles, CA 90058

Mav-Rik
3916 Eagle Park Blvd.
Los Angeles, CA 90065

FURTHER READING

There are more books available on the sport of bodybuilding today than at any other time in history, and more are being published every year. Beginning with general weight-training books, I wrote two that would be valuable to any bodybuilder—*Boyer & Valerie Coe's Weight Training Book* (Contemporary Books, 1982) with Boyer and Valerie Coe, and the *Complete Weight Training Book* (Anderson-World, 1976).

I can recommend two books specifically for women bodybuilders—Laura Combes' and my *Winning Women's Bodybuilding* (Contemporary, 1983), and *The Weider Book of Bodybuilding for Women* (Contemporary, 1981) by Betty and Joe Weider.

Every woman bodybuilder can also profit from reading this wide variety of recommended men's bodybuilding books—*Winning Bodybuilding* (Contemporary, 1976) by Franco Columbu; *Arnold: The Education of a Bodybuilder* (Simon and Schuster, 1977) by Arnold Schwarzenegger and Douglas Kent Hall; *Getting Strong, Looking Strong* (Atheneum, 1979) by Boyer Coe and Bob Summer; *Bodybuilding: The Weider Approach* (Contemporary, 1981) by Joe Weider; *Franco Columbu's Complete Book of Bodybuilding* (Contemporary, 1982) by Dr. Franco Columbu; and *The Weider System of Bodybuilding* (Contemporary, 1983) by Joe Weider and myself. I believe that my *The Gold's Gym Book of Bodybuilding* (Contemporary, 1983), written with Ken Sprague, is the single best bodybuilding instructional manual on the market.

There are nine anthologies of *Muscle & Fitness* magazine articles—*The Best of Joe Weider's Muscle & Fitness* series—published by Contemporary Books between 1981 and 1983. Two of these books are aimed at women, the rest at men, and all nine have good instructional material.

Pumping Iron (Simon and Schuster, 1974) by Charles Gaines and George Butler and *The Incredible Lou Ferrigno* (Simon and Schuster, 1982) by Lou Ferrigno and Douglas Kent Hall offer a good insight into the lives of champion bodybuilders.

Muscle & Fitness and *Flex* are the best bodybuilding magazines on the market for both men and women. They are available on newsstands, or you can obtain subscription information from Weider Health & Fitness, 21100 Erwin St., Woodland Hils, CA 91367. Other good bodybuilding magazines include *Muscle Mag International* (Unit One, 270 Rutherford Rd. S., Brampton, Ontario L6W 3K7, Canada), *Iron Man* (Box 10, Alliance, NE 69301), *Muscular Development* (Box 1707, York, PA 17405), and *Muscle Training Illustrated* (1665 Utica Ave., Brooklyn, NY 11234).

KEEP PUMPING IRON!

This is as far as I can take you in this beginning bodybuilding book. It's now up to you to continue reading and learning more about bodybuilding. But, above all else, it's up to you to get into the gym each day to train at 100 percent of your ability and to maintain a disciplined diet. In the final analysis *you* are totally responsible for your own success.

Keep pumping iron!

Glossary of Common Bodybuilding Terms

Aerobic Exercise—Long-lasting, low-intensity exercise that can be carried on within the body's ability to consume and process enough oxygen to support the activity. The word *aerobic* literally means "with air." Typical aerobic exercise activities are running, swimming, and cycling. *Aerobic* exercise leads to cardiorespiratory (heart-lung) fitness.

AFWB—The American Federation of Women Bodybuilders, the sports federation responsible for administering women's amateur bodybuilding in America. The AFWB is affiliated internationally with the IFBB (see **IFBB**).

AMDR—The Adult Minimum Daily Requirement(s) for various nutrients, as established by the U.S. Food and Drug Administration.

Anaerobic Exercise—High-intensity exercise that exceeds the body's aerobic capacity and builds up an oxygen debt. Because of its high intensity, *anaerobic* exercise can be continued for only a short time. A typical *anaerobic* exercise would be full-speed sprinting on a track.

APC—The American Physique Committee, Inc., the sports federation responsible for administering men's amateur bodybuilding in America. The *APC* is affiliated internationally with the IFBB (see **IFBB**).

Bar—The iron or steel shaft that forms the handle of a barbell or dumbbell. Barbell *bars* vary in length from about four to seven feet, while dumbbell *bars* are 12 to 16 inches long. *Bars* are usually one inch in diameter, and are often encased in a revolving sleeve (see **Sleeve**).

Barbell—This is the basic piece of equipment for weight training. It consists of a bar, sleeve, collars, and plates (see **Bar, Sleeve, Collar,** and **Plates**). The weight of an adjustable *barbell* without plates averages five pounds per foot of bar length. The weight of this basic *barbell* unit must be considered when adding plates to the bar to form a required training poundage (see **Poundage**). *Barbells* in large gyms are usually *fixed,* with the plates welded to the bars in a variety of poundages. These poundages are designated by numerals painted on the sides of the plates of each *barbell.*

BMR—The Basal Metabolic Rate, or the natural speed at which the body burns calories when at rest to provide its basic survival energy needs.

Bodybuilding—A subdivision of the general category of weight training (see **Weight Training**) in which the main objective is to change the appearance of the human body via weight training and nutrition. For most men and women, *bodybuilding* consists merely of reducing a fleshy area or two and/or building up one or two thin body parts. In its purest form, *bodybuilding* for men and women is a competitive sport both nationally and internationally in amateur and professional categories.

Bodysculpting—This term is occasionally used to mean *bodybuilding.*

Circuit Training—A specialized form of weight training that develops body strength and aerobic endurance simultaneously. In *circuit training,* a trainee plans a circuit of 10–20 exercises covering all of the body's major muscle groups, then proceeds around this circuit in order while resting minimally between sets. Many athletes use *circuit training* to improve their strength, muscle tone, and overall endurance in one type of workout.

Collar—The cylindrical metal clamp used to hold plates (see **Plates**) in position on a barbell. Usually these *collars* are secured in place with a *set screw* threaded through the *collar* and tightened against the bar with a wrench. *Inside collars* keep plates from sliding inward and injuring a trainee, while *outside collars* keep the plates from sliding off the end of the bar. For safety, you should never lift a barbell unless the *collars* are tightly fastened in place.

Couples' Competition—Also called "Mixed Pairs' Competition," this is a new form of bodybuilding competition in which man/woman teams compete against each other. Couples' competition is becoming very popular with bodybuilding fans all over the world.

Cut—A term used to denote a well-defined bodybuilder (see **Definition**). Usually this is a complimentary term, such as in saying, "He's *really* cut up for this show!"

Definition—This term is used to denote an absence of body fat in a bodybuilding competitor, so that every muscle is fully delineated or *defined.* When a competitor has achieved ideal *definition,* his or her muscles will show striations, or individual fibers along a muscle (see **Striations**). *Definition* is also called *muscularity.*

Density—The hardness of muscle tissue, denoting complete muscularity, even to the point where fat within a muscle has been eliminated.

Dumbbell—This is simply a shorter version of a barbell, which is intended for use in one hand, or more commonly with equally weighted *dumbbells* in each hand. All of the principal parts and terminology of a barbell are the same for a *dumbbell.*

Exercise—Used as a noun, this is the actual weight training movement being done (e.g., a bench press or a squat). An *exercise* is often called a *movement.* Used as a verb, *exercise* is the act of undertaking physical work recreationally and for health reasons with weight training or any number of other forms of *exercise* (e.g., running, playing softball, etc.).

Flexibility—A suppleness of muscles and connective tissue that allows any man or woman to move his or her limbs and torso over a complete—or even exaggerated—range of motion.

Hypertrophy—The growth in size and strength of any skeletal muscle.

IFBB—The International Federation of Bodybuilders, which was founded in 1946 by Ben and Joe Weider. It is the parent international federation overseeing worldwide men's and women's amateur and professional bodybuilding. More than 115 national bodybuilding federations are affiliated with the *IFBB,* making bodybuilding the world's seventh most popular sport.

Intensity—The degree of difficulty built into weight training exercise. *Intensity* can be increased by adding resistance (see **Resistance**), increasing the number of repetitions done of an exercise (see **Repetition**), or by decreasing the rest interval between sets (see **Rest Interval** and **Set**). The greater the *inten-*

sity of bodybuilding exercise placed on a muscle, the greater will be that muscle's rate of hypertrophy.

Judging Rounds—In the internationally accepted IFBB system of bodybuilding judging, three *judging rounds* are contested, plus a final posedown in which the top five contestants compete in a free posing manner for added points. In Round One each bodybuilder is viewed standing relaxed facing his/her front, left side, back, and right side to the judges. Round Two consists of a set of standardized compulsory poses, while Round Three is devoted to creative individual free posing to each contestant's own choice of music.

Lifting Belt—A leather belt four to six inches wide at the back that is worn around the waist to protect a trainee's lower back and abdomen from injuries. The six-inch belt can be used in training, but only the four-inch belt can be used in weightlifting competition (see **Weightlifting**).

Mass—The size or fullness of muscles. Massiveness is highly prized in bodybuilding competition, especially for men.

Muscularity—Another term for definition (see **Definition**).

Nutrition—The various practices of taking food into the human body. Bodybuilders have made a science of *nutrition* by applying it to add muscle mass or to totally strip fat from their bodies to achieve optimum muscle definition.

Olympic Barbell—A highly specialized and finely machined barbell used in weightlifting competition. An *Olympic barbell* weighs 20 kilograms (slightly less than 45 pounds), and each of its collars weighs 2½ kilograms (5.5 pounds).

Olympic Lifting—A form of competitive weightlifting included in the Olympic Games since the revival of the modern Olympics at

Athens in 1896. Until 1972 this form of weightlifting consisted of three lifts: the press, snatch, and clean and jerk. Because of officiating difficulties, however, the press was dropped from use following the 1972 Olympic Games, leaving the snatch, and the clean and jerk as the two competitive Olympic lifts.

PHA—An abbreviation for *peripheral heart action,* in which each skeletal muscle acts as an auxiliary heart by milking blood past one-way valves in the arterial system. Without *PHA,* the heart itself would have difficulty circulating blood. *PHA* is also a term assigned to a system of circuit training (see **Circuit Training**) in which shorter series of five or six exercises are used in circuits.

Plates—The flat discs pierced with holes in the middle that are fitted on barbells and dumbbells to increase the weight of these apparatus. *Plates* are made of cast metal or vinyl-covered concrete. They come in a wide range of graduated weights from as little as 1¼ pounds to over 100 pounds each.

Poundage—The actual weight of a barbell, dumbbell, or weight machine resistance used in an exercise.

Powerlifting—A form of competitive weightlifting using three lifts: the squat, the bench press, and the deadlift. The sport is contested nationally and internationally. Unlike in Olympic lifting, special women's competitions are held in *powerlifting.*

Proportion—A competitive bodybuilding term referring to the size relationships between various body parts. A contestant with good *proportions* will have no over- or underdeveloped muscle groups.

Pyramidding—A technique of gradually increasing weights lifted while decreasing the number of reps performed. For example, in doing three *pyramidded* sets of an exercise, you might begin the first set with 100 pounds and do 8 reps, then 110 pounds for 6 reps, and finish with 120 pounds for 4 reps.

Repetition—Often abbreviated as *rep,* this is each individual full cycle of an exercise from the starting point of the movement to the midpoint and back again to the starting point.

Resistance—As with *poundage,* this is the actual weight being used in an exercise.

Rest Interval—The pause between sets of an exercise (see **Set**) during which the worked muscles are allowed to partially recuperate before the succeeding set is begun. *Rest intervals* vary from as little as 10–15 seconds to as much as five minutes. An average *rest interval* should be 60 seconds.

Routine—Sometimes called a *program* or *schedule,* this is the complete accumulation of exercises, sets, and reps, done in one training session. A routine is usually repeated two or three times each week.

Set—A distinct grouping of repetitions, followed by a brief rest interval and another *set.* Usually, several *sets* are done for each exercise in a training program.

Sleeve—A hollow metal tube fitted over the bar of a barbell. The *sleeve* allows a bar to rotate more easily in your hands. Ordinarily, grooved *knurlings* are scored in the *sleeve* to aid in gripping the barbell when the hands have become sweaty during a training session.

Spotters—Training partners who stand by as a safety factor to prevent you from being pinned under a heavy barbell. *Spotters* are particularly necessary when you are doing Bench Presses.

Steroids—Prescriptive, artificial male hormones that some bodybuilders use to increase muscle mass. Anabolic *steroids* are very dangerous drugs, however, and we do not recommend that anyone use them.

Stretching—A type of exercise program used to promote body flexibility. It involves assuming and then holding postures in which certain muscle groups and body joints are stretched.

Striations—This is the ultimate degree of muscle definition. When a muscle mass like the pectoral is fully defined, it will have myriad small grooves across it, almost as if a cat had repeatedly scratched the wax surface of a statue's pectoral muscles. These tiny, muscular details are called *striations*.

Supplements—Concentrated vitamins, minerals, and protein, usually in tablet/capsule or powder form. Food *supplements* are widely used by competitive bodybuilders, weightlifters, and athletes to optimize their overall nutritional programs.

Symmetry—In competitive bodybuilding parlance, this is the shape or general outline of the body, as if it was seen in silhouette. *Symmetry* is enhanced in both male and female bodybuilders by a wide shoulder structure; a small waist-hip structure; small knees, ankles, and wrists; and large muscle volumes surrounding these small joints.

Vascularity—The appearance of surface veins and arteries in any bodybuilder who has achieved a low level of body fat. Women tend to have *vascularity* primarily in their arms, while male bodybuilders can have surface *vascularity* all over their bodies.

Weight—Another term for *poundage* or *resistance*. Sometimes this term is used to generally refer to the apparatus (barbell, dumbbell, etc.) being used in an exercise, versus the exact poundage being utilized.

Weight Class—So that smaller athletes are not overwhelmed by larger ones, competitive bodybuilding and weightlifting utilize *weight classes.* In women's bodybuilding, the classes (at the time of writing this book) were: under 52½ kg. (114 lbs.) and over 52½ kg., while men's bodybuilding weight classes are set at: 70 kg. (154 lbs.), 80 kg. (176 lbs.), 90 kg. (198 lbs.), and over 90 kg. or heavyweight. Powerlifting and Olympic lifting are contested in a much wider variety of weight classes. Converted to pounds from international metric equivalents, these are: 114, 123, 132, 148, 165, 181, 198, 220, 242, 275, and over 275 pounds.

Weightlifting—The subdivision of weight training in which men and women compete in weight classes both nationally and internationally to see who can lift the heaviest weights for single repetitions in prescribed exercises. Two types of *weightlifting—Olympic lifting* and *powerlifting*—are contested.

Weight Training—The various acts of using resistance training equipment to exercise the body or for competitive purposes.

Workout—A weight training session. "To work out" is to undertake a weight training session.

Index

N

O

P

R

S

T

U–V

W–Z